Again, A Time Machine:
from distribution to archive

Edited by Gavin Everall and Jane Rolo
Book Works, 2012

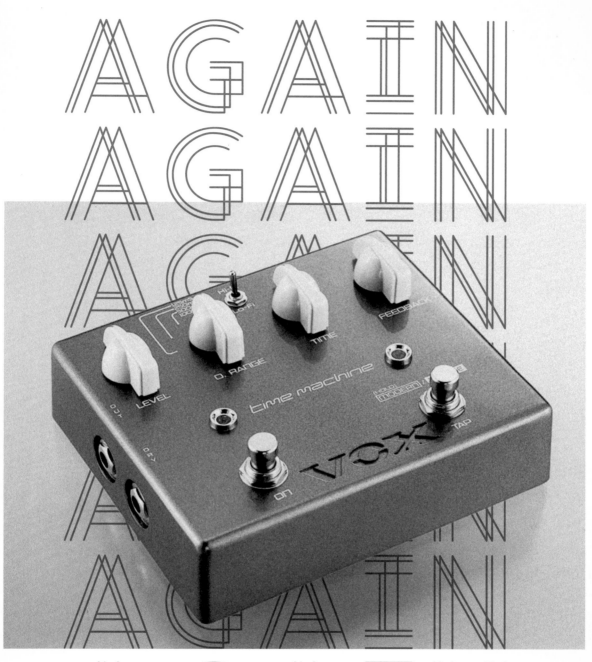

Contents

Where do you see Book Works beginning?

JR

… is that the first question?

GE

… No, I've written it down. Shall I read it out? I only have one, as I wanted just a conversation.

JR

I thought the first question was 'Where do you see Book Works beginning?'

GE

No, that was just a prompt. I know we're never going to answer that. Shall I just read it out?

Beginning 1: Again

GE

One of the themes of the exhibition *Again, A Time Machine* — inevitably for a show that looks at our own history — has been the play and movement of time. And this has intersected with, or been book-ended by this haphazard notion of archive on the one hand and a fluid idea of distribution on the other. It's not clear what comes first, distribution or archive, in the sense that one publishes and distributes in order to reclaim, recoup and archive. You put it out, before looking for it again. And this presents different starting points for a conversation that looks at this exhibition and thinking about Book Works.[1]

---

1   *Again, A Time Machine* was a touring exhibition that changed and reinvented itself as it moved from venue to venue. Based on new commissions, the project explored ideas of both distribution and archive, whilst playing with the use of words, notions of time, and taking a heretical approach to the authority of the archive. Commissioned work expanded and dissipated, archival commissions were re-presented, and new work was manifest as ephemera, discursive events, performance, film, and new publications. It was organised by Book Works, with Eastside Projects, Birmingham; Motto, Berlin; Spike Island, Bristol; White Columns, New York; The Showroom, London; and SPACE, London, in 2011–12. Book Works and collaborating organisations commissioned major new work from Dora García, *The Happy Hypocrite*, Stewart Home, Jonathan Monk, Laure Prouvost, Sarah Pierce and Slavs & Tatars. In total over ninety-five artists, writers and organisations participated in the exhibition.

JR

As I see it in relation to this project, there are two beginnings really: the historic beginning — important because Rob and I have been here from the start and there is that continuity and memory that goes back to the very beginning.[2] And the other possible beginning is this project, which is perhaps more interesting to start with, because the beginning of *Again, A Time Machine* came out of thinking about our twenty-fifth anniversary in 2009, and some ideas of past, present and future that we tried to encapsulate in the film we produced with Gilly Booth at hijack.[3] We tried to tease out the essence of what we thought the first twenty-five years were in five minutes, and we found that quite problematic: the things you leave out suddenly became as important as the things you want in. At the same time as wanting to capture a moment in time, and having to edit out most of our history, we also decided to open up and organise our archive through an online digital presence, as a resource on our website. So, at the same moment of editing out we were also starting to rediscover. And each project informed the other. I suppose it's like looking in the attic at all the junk you put up there, and shining a torch in some corners but actually knowing you're probably more interested in what's in the dark corner, and knowing that there is always something else to uncover.

GE

Part of this problem you mention, is the idea of being fixed. It's difficult to know which beginning to follow, because in a sense each one fixes Book Works, either in the past — historically, or in the present — without history. Maybe one of the ways to look at Book Works is in the way it works, its processes, methods, how it negotiates fixed positions. Artists' books, for example, is a term we embrace but don't really have a definition for.

JR

Yes, I'm very against trying to pin things down, either with meaning or in time, because I think that the moment you fix it, something dislodges it. And I've always been quite reluctant to define what an artist's book is for similar reasons, because I think the minute you define it, you immediately want to do something outside of the scope of what an artist's book is. It's as if you are cornering yourself, or being asked to come up with a position. I always thought that they are all just books. Or all just works.

And now, even defining the books as being by artists becomes problematic because we work with people who want to be called something else, for example, writers or editors. This cropped up in the book we're doing with Brian Catling and Iain Sinclair.[4] Brian is described as an artist in the credits, and he's come back to ask if he can also be called a poet. So the minute you define someone, or define an artist's book, it closes it down rather than opening it up.

JB

And Book Works has always tried to open things up and reveal things. Because it's not just artists' books we do, it's artists' projects in lots of different forms: performances, installations, ephemera, events, our studio practice.

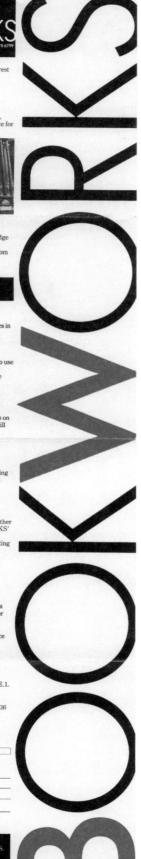

GE

People don't seem to understand this in relation to books or, 'what we should be doing' as a publisher. There is confusion about why, if you produce artists' books, you are doing exhibitions, or spoken word or performance.

JR

It does free you up in terms of the opportunities you can offer artists. Sometimes it might not be appropriate to do a book, but it might be better to do a spoken word performance, or an intervention of some sort. And it's through those different types of projects that you get to know an artist better, and you build a confidence on both sides that allows you to perhaps do another project, perhaps a book, in the future.

GE

Was this approach there at the start of Book Works?

JR

One of the first models for Book Works came from visiting the Center for Book Arts in New York.[5] They had an exhibition space, as well as a large workshop space where they offered different types of practical print and bookmaking workshops and classes. They didn't have a bookshop, but

2   Book Works was founded in 1984, by the current Directors Rob Hadrill and Jane Rolo, with Pella Erskine Tulloch, Vanessa Marshall and Jen Lindsay. It was based at Arch No. 3, Green Dragon Court, Borough Market, London SE1.
3   *Book Works Film*, directed and produced by hijack and Book Works, 2009.
4   Brian Catling and Iain Sinclair, *Several Clouds Colliding*, co-published by Book Works and the Swedenborg Archive, London, 2012.
5   Other equally important influences, based in New York at the time, were the artists' bookshop, Printed Matter, and the archive and performance space, Franklin Furnace.

they had a sort of social scene — they did talks and everything, and that's what we wanted to replicate in London. But given the price of rent, it all got reduced in scale, so what was a big open plan warehouse space in New York became two derelict railway arches in Borough Market — they weren't even the size of arches that everyone else had, they were tiny.

At the start we concentrated on a gallery. Coming from a craft background — the group of us who started Book Works had all trained as bookbinders — we saw an opportunity for exhibiting artists' books, but after a while it became obvious that there really wasn't very much of the sort of stuff that we wanted to show. There was historical stuff, for instance, those conceptual art books produced in the '60s and '70s, and unique, one-off books that were more like objects, that occupied a space between sculpture and craft. But we weren't finding much contemporary work that appealed to us. There wasn't that much of an opportunity to publish it, and we realised the only way to do exhibitions with work we were interested in, was to start commissioning it ourselves.

GE

There does seem to be something interesting in the idea of binding being the basis for Book Works, even if there was a move away from the history and the aesthetics of craft. Binding seems to act as a metaphor, and describes a history of collaborative practice. Also, from the start you had a studio and a bookbinding practice?

JR

That's always run alongside and in collaboration with the publishing.[6] It's important to note that we didn't start off as publishers, we started off as a commissioning organisation that was particularly interested in books. In the early days we also used Borough Market as an outdoor gallery space, because the arches were so small, and so unsuitable for anything much because they were damp — difficult conditions to show books in. The artists we were working with were practising across different media and so there were always these parallel activities of exhibiting, and later producing, books and sometimes producing work that was more event based.

KDF

Looking at Book Works' archive, and the material from Borough Market, it seems that the space was very similar to an artist-led gallery or project space. How did the commissioning process work? Was there a willingness on the part of people you were working with to develop something that wasn't defined? And how were things funded?

JR

There were always little bits of money, but never very much. To be honest I can't even remember whether there was enough to pay the artists who had shows anything at all. That idea of paying a fee was just emerging in the '80s. It wasn't standard practice, because the work was often ready-made and then shown. And it wasn't as if the people running galleries were helping to instigate new work all the time.

There was an important community of people working in similar ways at that time, like Coracle, who had a very strong publishing arm already but who also curated exhibitions.[7] They were producing some really exciting work and everyone used to trek down to Camberwell to see their shows. They were very important.

The main difference between us and Coracle was that they seemed to be coming out of a more literary/poetic tradition, publishing hand-made books in quite small editions. The very first book that Book Works published was with a performance artist, Silvia Ziranek, and we printed it in two editions: one of which was printed offset in a large edition and sold quite cheaply. The idea was that you could find it in any bookshop that would take it, next to a catalogue by Silvia. The other was a limited edition version of the book — hand-bound, with a signed and numbered screen print.

6   Book Works Studio operates as a specialist bindery pro-
     ducing boxes, portfolios, specialist editions and binding
     for a range of artists and organisations, including Douglas
     Gordon, Damien Hirst, Anish Kapoor, Beatriz Milhazes,
     Chris Ofili among many others.
7   Coracle was founded in 1975 by Simon Cutts and worked
     from bases in London, Norfolk, Italy, Liverpool and Ire-
     land. Cutts was joined by New England book artist and
     writer Erica Van Horn as co-director of Coracle in 1989.

GE

It was a cookbook wasn't it?

JR

Yes. It was a cookbook, *Very Food*.[8]

GE

Do you think that was a provocative thing to do, as a small artists' book space, to publish in this way, in a large, machine-printed edition.

A MUST - SEMINAL, POLEMIC, DOMESTIC POLITICALE - IN SHORT COMME CHEZ NOUS, THE ONLY BOOK FOR THE CONSCIOUS COOK.

JR

Yes, maybe. We didn't want to do just what other people were doing, and we were influenced by what we'd seen in New York, at the Center for Book Arts, and at Printed Matter too.

GE

We put a letter from Simon and Erica to Book Works in one of the *Again, A Time Machine* leaflets. Was that in response to the first book?

JR

Maybe, although that letter was in response to our first Arts Council application and the request for support … Simon and Erica are very good cooks. And I don't think that anyone at Book Works has ever been linked to fine wining and dining. So maybe it's a veiled reference to that …[9]

GE

To go back to Brian Catling. We are doing a new project with him and he also did one of our very first projects. Did he define himself as a poet and artist when he first approached us? Did he see Book Works as a space for writing and poetry or a space for art?

JR

I'm not sure, or whether it matters. He has done several projects with us over the years. The first was a site-specific project on an old sailing boat — the *Kathleen & May* — near Borough Market, that was a result of a very early open submission. And of course Brian performed the role — he came dressed as a sort of tramp, and sat in the garden of Southwark Cathedral that we looked out on for what seemed liked most of the day. He looked a bit odd and kept staring up at us and eventually came to the door, banged on it and shoved over this great lump of a package that was his proposal. We thought about trying to keep him out, but I remember thinking 'this isn't one of the local winos' and that he might be an artist, and that I might even know him. So, you can sort of take your pick whether he was an artist, or a wino, or a poet, but he was already writing and doing quite a lot of big sculptural projects, and performances too.[10]

dear bookworks,

i think that your work
is complitly absurd and
'inframince' like they say in
france. it's maybe better
for you to stop the
production and beginnig
to learn cooking!!!!
with love!!!!

workforeyetodo.
conspirator of the system.

8   Silvia Ziranek, *Very Food*, Book Works, London, 1987.
9   Workfortheeyetodo, a bookshop run by Simon Cutts, Maggie Smith, and Erica Van Horn, originally 152 Narrow Street, London, 1993–95, then Hanbury Street, London, 1995–98.
10 Brian Catling, *Site Works II*, 1988; *Book Works New Work*, 1990; *The Stumbling Block, Its Index*, 1990; *The Reading Room*, 1994; *Scroll*, 1994; *The Blindings*, 1995; *Scroll Revisited*, 2011; *Several Clouds Colliding*, with Iain Sinclair, co-published with the Swedenborg Archive.

GE
So you knew his work?

JR
Yes. I knew his work already.

GE
But you had no idea of what the proposal was?

JR
No.

GE
And, that's been a key element of Book Works commissioning — that stepping into the unknown and taking on the unfamiliar?

JR
Yes. Taking a calculated risk, well not even that calculated, just taking a risk that the artist is going to produce or do something as good as the projects that they've done before. Or taking on projects with artists who are quite new to the scene, that haven't done a lot, haven't really got anything to show for themselves yet. One of the nice things about being non-profit is that you can behave in a different way than a more commercial publisher. Obviously the subsidies that we get through grants help us take those risks.

GE
But those risks predate the main source of funding? That ambition has been there from the start?

JR
Yes, although in a way the risks were less then, because we had nothing to lose. It just felt like there were artists who you were excited about, and we proposed to do something together.

GE
We've mentioned open submissions, maybe this is a good moment to talk more about the commissioning process: who we approach and how we do it. It seems to be a process that involves stepping outside of working with people who've made books already?

PS
Did you originally work with people who had made books before?

JR

Yes. Originally we approached people who were making books — we did a show with all the books of Richard Hamilton and Dieter Roth.[11] Part of it was at Book Works, and part of it was at a gallery bookshop that was popular at the time, Nigel Greenwood. But we also worked with people like Langlands and Bell, who hadn't produced books, and actually never really did produce books for the shows we did, just objects that somehow shared that space with books. We picked up on artists like that, and people like Ian Tyson, who ran his own press, Tetrad Press, and Ron King of Circle Press, and through him Art in Ruins, partly to show their new work but also because they were friends — a bit more like the Coracle model, where Simon and Erica produced their own books, but then invited other people to make books with them. However, we also worked with many younger artists making books for the first time, and by using the area around Borough Market, others who worked with sound, sculpture, film, performance etc.[12]

FROM THE RUINS

KDF

So were these friends or people you knew, or people who came to Book Works?

JR

A mixture. From both the book world and art world who we knew.

JB

But there must have been a point when you'd established a network, and then stepped outside of it, and people came to Book Works with proposals?

11   *Editions*, Hansjörg Mayer, April to May 1986, in conjunction with Nigel Greenwood Books.

12   Circle Press was set up in 1967 by Ron King, a printmaker and book artist, along with a group of like-minded artists, including Ian Tyson and John Christie, all interested in working and exploring the printed form and book art. Ian Tyson established Tetrad Press in 1970 to publish his own artists' books, and ed.it, in 1995. Art in Ruins was formed in 1984 by artists Hannah Vowles and Glyn Banks, as a collaborative interventionist practice in art and architecture, staging exhibitions, and publishing texts. In 1985 Art in Ruins collaborated with Book Works on an exhibition *From the Ruins*, and the launch of *Work from Common Knowledge* by Glyn Banks, John Colman and Hannah Vowles, produced by Circle Press, 1985.

JR

I think that tipping point came a bit later. The open submission came first of all. We had a couple called *Site Works*, for site-specific projects around the Borough Market area. This was the project with Brian Catling, with performance and sculptural works on the old boat and an archaeological site in the market, and with Cornelia Parker where she made hundreds of tiny lead cathedrals that were suspended from an outdoor archway by the gallery, and a film by Langlands and Bell, projected outside.[13] Then we decided that we'd carry on that idea of opening up to people who we didn't know, through the open submissions. Because remember, we weren't really part of the gallery scene, we were part of the DIY culture of little galleries and artist-run spaces popping up here and there, and if we were part of anything we were part of that.

When we formalised the open submissions process to be more about the publishing side of things, it was to provide a way of finding out what was going on further afield. We didn't have any money to travel, we weren't curators being given a travel grant to go to America or Europe or anywhere, so it was a way of getting artists to come to us.

GE

Do you think that there is a certain type of artist you like to work with, or a certain type of work?

JR

I don't think I can answer that. I think that has to be answered by someone who sees all of our books. Of course, even though you see each project as a completely new thing — a new set of issues with completely different content — there is a strand, an aesthetic maybe, that runs through everything.

GE

Just to go back to the idea of risk and of finding the unknown: what do you look for in a proposal? Do you see the finished project in the proposal? And what is the editing process? Although I guess you didn't call it that in the early days.

JR

No, we didn't. We certainly wouldn't have called ourselves editors. We wouldn't call ourselves publishers. We would have called ourselves collaborators, and the process is really one of working through the germs of an idea, and shaping it, but without necessarily knowing where it is going. We're not interested in proposals that are finished, or even ones that we just 'get'. I'm more interested in something that is both unexpected, unknown, and that we don't really understand. Then the process is really interesting. I don't really see the point in publishing something you've seen before, or something that's finished in the artist's mind before you've even worked on it.

GE

Do you think that there is a particular method or manner of working with the artists we commission, that draws out the projects?

JR

Well, sometimes it's just the result of a conversation. One of the first open submissions we did was the *New Writing Series*, which was guest edited by Michael Bracewell.[14] We'd worked with him before, and I'd gone to hear him give a talk somewhere, perhaps when he was still working at the British Council in the early 1990s. What Michael was saying, and what a lot of people have been saying since, was how excited he felt by the idea that the art world was the true home of the avant-garde and counterculture, rather than the more literary world where he was producing his novels. I thought that was quite exciting, and when we were thinking about the *New Writing Series*, and this idea of, what I think we were calling then, a sort of 'no man's land between art and literature', he seemed to be a good person to get involved with that series and with helping to select the artists. So, some of the things we've done have been developed through other people's interests, or tastes, or shaping. But there is something that runs through it all that must be to do with me and Rob, and all the other people that work here. This again is enriched by the guest curators and editors we have worked with, who bring new ideas and connections with them, for example Matthew Higgs, Maria Fusco, or, more recently, Stewart Home or Nina Power. Each has a distinct way of working with artists, that we can build on, and that helps keep the process fresh and exciting to be part of.[15]

GE

And the selection of those people came about either through open submission or through conversations. Conversation does seem to play quite an important part ...

13 *Site Works I*, Langlands and Bell, Richard Layzell and Cornelia Parker, 1986; *Site Works II*, Brian Catling, Jo Stockham, Stefan Szcelkun, 1988.

14 *New Writing Series*, edited by Michael Bracewell: Jeremy Millar, *Confessions*, 1994; David Shrigley, *Err*, 1995; Deborah Levy, *Diary of a Steak*, 1997; Steve Beard, *Perfumed Head*, 1998; Virgil Tracey, *Under Hempel's Sofa*, 1998; Emma Kay, *Worldview*, 1999; Adam Chodzko, *Romanov*, 2002; Lucy Kimbell, *Audit*, 2002; Lawrence Norfolk and Neal White, *Ott's Sneeze*, 2002; Michael Bracewell & Linder, *I Know Where I'm Going: A Guide to Morecambe & Heysham*, 2003.

15 *Publish and Be Damned*, edited by Matthew Higgs, Open House, 1998–99; *Access / Excess*, edited by Stephan Kalmár, Open House, 1999–2000; *Warms Seas*, edited by Craig Martin, Open House, 2000–01; *Opus Projects*, edited by Lisa Panting, 2000–05; *Infra Thin Projects*, curated by Mark Beasley, 2004–05; *Scape Specific*, edited by Sara Wajid, 2004–05; *Fabrications*, edited by Gerrie Van Noord, 2006–09; *Singular Sociology*, edited by Nav Haq, 2008–09; *The Happy Hypocrite*, edited by Maria Fusco, 2008–10; *Semina*, edited by Stewart Home, 2009–11; *Time Machine*, edited by Francesco Pedraglio, 2011–12; and *Common Objectives*, edited by Nina Power, 2012–13.

J. MILLAR   D. SHRIGLEY

JR

Michael's was a direct invitation. Then we formalised it, and that's always the trouble, the older you get everything becomes slightly more formalised and slightly less casual. By the time Matthew Higgs came to Book Works there was an open call process for guest curators in place and we selected him.

KDF

As part of the archiving process I've read quite a lot of people's applications, and it's interesting to see how the ideas evolve over time and develop through being here. For example, Mark Beasley's conversations start with the artists who he wants to invite, and their ideas slightly adapt, even if it's not necessarily what is produced. It's being discussed, then adapted, then edited, then changed, then filtered, and that seems to be how these conversations, these relationships seem to evolve as well.[16]

JR

It's open-ended. Maybe that's because a book has a longer life than an exhibition. Not only do you have a longer time to work with them on the process of producing the book, you also have a longer aftermath because the books don't go away, they are around for a long time.

KDF

I was struck by your ambivalence to the archive. There was an openness to interpretation that allowed me to delve into it without thinking that there was an onus, or a certain type of material that I should be looking for, or how to deal with it.

JR

I think it's less an ambivalence, and more that we're interested in creating something new. What I was interested in with *Make the Living Look Dead*, is the relationship of new material to the archive. It was mad in a way — to ask for even more stuff — but I like the relationship it had and how it changed a historic moment, and it made you wonder about future possibilities.[17]

GE

At the time of the site-specific installations did you think about the future archive?

JR

No, we just produced. If anything, we just thought let's shove that in that box. Having said that, I think some artists and curators we worked with, were consciously thinking about it and aware of archiving themselves. For instance, every time we got a fax from Douglas Gordon, it had the same heading, same typeface — similarly with Joseph Kosuth. Even in the more recent emails we've had from Jonathan Monk, you recognise that sort of style, that way of writing, that signing off …

GE

… sent with the wink of an eye.[18]

JR

They were always the same, and I now understand that they were positioning themselves maybe as a brand, or more with a view to archiving their own documentation.

KDF

There is a difference between whether you are producing something to be re-evaluated, or producing material to document. With Douglas's letters to you, they are a work aren't they?

JR

Yes, they are a work and they have a value, certainly in terms of his own archive, and our own. But they also explain a process, a way of working that is revealing.

KDF

I wonder if he produced them in duplicate?

JR

I'm sure he did. Certainly the text pieces were mailed to a number of people — lots of people were wondering about green eyes. Actually, I don't think that Douglas even has green eyes.[19]

The other person who had this canny awareness of the archive was Matthew Higgs. When he came here, the first thing he did was read everything. He read everything that was in the Book Works office — every scrap of paper — to get an overall picture of Book Works as an organisation.

London, July 16th, 1993.

Dear Jane,

From the moment you read these words, until you meet someone with green eyes.

Yours,

Douglas Gordon

16 As part of the archiving process, Book Works has developed a new website and digital archive that now includes material ranging from finished works to ephemera, correspondence, photographs and manuscripts providing an insight into the working processes of both the publishing and studio sections of the organisation. The archive and website have been developed by Karen Di Franco, Digital Archivist and James Brook, Sales & Distribution Manager, 1995–2012, in collaboration with Camberwell College of Arts, University of Arts London, with support from the Knowledge Transfer Programme scheme and Arts Council England. Designed by Yes Studio London.

17 *Make the Living Look Dead* was a new commission for *Again, A Time Machine*. We asked thirty artists who we'd previously worked to produce a new contribution on A4 paper for the archive — either something ephemeral, or something from the time of the original project, or to make a new work. It was displayed alongside a Book Works archive presented in the form of a moving image work and sound archive, compiled by Karen Di Franco and James Brook.

18 *Sent with the wink of an eye*, Jonathan Monk, artist's pages for *Again, A Time Machine*, edited by Gavin Everall and Jane Rolo, Book Works, London, 2012.

19 *From the moment you read these words to the moment you meet someone with green eyes.* Text by Douglas Gordon, 1993.

He had already started producing his publishing project, *Imprint 93*, in small editions, and I always got a copy in the mail, as did a lot of other people. What I hadn't realised, as I just thought that this was a generous gesture to send work through the post for free, was that he was putting some copies on one side, archiving them if you like, and that complete sets would later be sold to important art and library collections. And at Book Works we never had that awareness that there was any intrinsic value in any of the ephemera, or any of the process or maybe even in the finished material. It was just there — you sold it or it sat in a box. And it was only when we realised how long we'd been going that we thought that some of this material did have a value.

GE

What about the other end, when it comes out of the box and you sell it. What about distribution? It's not just about selling is it? It's about more than that …

JR

Yes, it's about the community, the audience, the reader. I think with the early publicity we used to send out, we called it dissemination, which was more in the spirit of trying to get things out to a wider audience or readership.

PS

And what about bookshops, book fairs, and galleries? How have they changed? What were the first ones that Book Works was involved with? When you made *Very Food*, how did you get it out there? You said you thought of it as a book that could go into any bookshop.

JR

There weren't very many bookshops or galleries with shops around then. So there were in fact very few bookshops that would take it. There were some independent bookshops, like Nigel Greenwood Gallery, and Compendium was just about still going. Workfortheeyetodo came later. We went on the road with Silvia, and she did performance readings and tastings, in five or six venues around the country, and at the Nigel Greenwood Gallery. We had quite a strong relationship there — Ann Gallagher who was running the bookshop, was very supportive. And it was a way of us being in the West End, just off Cork Street. Nigel was very keen on a younger generation, who weren't necessarily going to be his gallery artists, but that somehow gave a connection to the art scene.

GE

And what about the book fairs that have sprung up now, how do they compare to fairs in 1984?

JR

There were very few then. There was a small press fair in Vauxhall, London, which was great actually, because it wasn't just art books, it had all sorts of bizarre and interesting things, such as trans-gender magazines, black magic, anarchists and political groups, all sorts of things. So there was that, and then the international one was Frankfurt. We had a stand at Frankfurt from quite early on. In the beginning we shared a stand with Imschoot, which was a Belgium-based artists' book publisher and they were good company, because they were publishing American heavyweights like Dan Graham, Joseph Kosuth, John Baldessari etc., and that seemed very international to us. They introduced us to book buyers and collectors who we hadn't come across before. We also always asked to be near Coracle, and in fact there was a small grouping of visual art publishers that formed a community within this massive book fair at Frankfurt. That carried on into another generation that included Christoph Keller and Revolver books, Sternberg Press, and JRP Editions (now JRP Ringier), so for us it had different manifestations at different moments. Now of course there is a proliferation of artists' book fairs, all around the globe.

GE
You also self-organised fairs. You did something in New York in a hotel …

JR
That's right, to an extent. There was a guy called Rik Gadella, and he set up these artists' book fairs, called …

JB
The ArtistBook International …[20]

JR
… and it took place in different hotels in different cities. The Waldorf in New York, I think, and some posh hotel on the Rue de Rivoli in Paris.

KDF
Did they know about it, or did he just hire a room and do it?

JR
No, they knew. We were the 'light relief', with Imschoot and Coracle, and one other publisher, I think. Each publisher was allocated a bedroom, and the four of us used

BOOKWORKS: HAPPY NEW YEAR FROM IMSCHOOT, UITGEVERS, WITH FOND RECOLLECTIONS OF OUR SHARED FAIRS! KAATJE & Piet (ALSO FOR CORNELIA) :)

20   ArtistBook International, 1994–2007, organised by Rik Gadella dedicated exclusively to artists' books. Starting in Paris 1994, following events were organised in New York 1995, Cologne 1996, New York 1997 and again in Paris from 2005 onwards.

to share a room together, because we were the cheaper end of this luxury artists' book world that the fair promoted. So there were publishers selling books for £1000 and upwards, and our books were selling for £10–£20. The organiser liked us, and always gave us good deals, because we brought in the artists, and the younger curators and designers, and we created the party.

JB

Some of the first Frankfurt Book Fairs that I did, in 1995 and 1996 we shared this tiny stand with Imschoot. There were always good people coming, new customers, new bookshops, libraries and individuals. And that's a marked shift to the last Frankfurt, which was really quiet. Frankfurt went off the boil for us, people were getting their information in different ways, which coincided with all these new smaller art book fairs. Actually people were very disaffected by Frankfurt, and the people that we'd grown up with had started going in a more commercial direction, or stopped going. There is now much more interest in the smaller, specialist art book fairs, but there was a time when it was really important to be in Frankfurt, and to be seen there.

JR

It gave us a validation. If you were there, it meant you had survived another year.

GE

I think it is interesting that by our last one, in 2006, we ended up on a crossroads on one of the aisles, a prime position with Vice Versa, JRP, Sternberg, and Edition Fink. And I think that the only publisher out of that grouping — with whom we had a shared interest at the time — that now goes to the new art book fairs is Book Works.

JR

Is that because they have distributors that go on their behalf?

GE

I don't think so. Some of the fairs have no distributors, like Pa/per View, or Salon Lite. I think it's because they've gone down a more commercial route.

JB

Book Works has always had a different attitude towards distribution. We've always believed in a multi-pronged approach, that you may well have a distributor, but you also have to sell your-self, talk to people and engage with your readership, without relying solely on distributors.

GE

It's also to do with the relationship that we have with not just emerging artists, but also with new bookshops, self-publishers and art organisations, and there is an ongoing relation-ship between Book Works as a more institutional organisation and other self-publishers, and smaller project spaces.

JB

Frankfurt was about the ambitions of Book Works at the time. The goal was to get into main-stream bookshops, and not just be marginalised into an art ghetto.

JR

Frankfurt was set up as a book fair for selling foreign rights, and artists' books don't fit naturally into that model. Now there all these dedicated art book fairs that are more focused. But perhaps it does still ghettoise you, though in a bigger pond. There was something I liked about being in Frankfurt, about it being every sort of possible book, about being among everything.

GE

There is something about self-publishing and the smaller fairs, which has a limited horizon. It tends to define its territory and stay within it. And Book Works has always tried to step into different territories.

JR

Thinking about what we used to do and what's different between now and then: bookshops then would have been happy to do a display of all our books, so we used to be offered the window of Dillons, or Waterstones in Covent Garden, and then came the 'three for two' deal, and the end of free shop-window displays, and now we know it's all sewn up by the bigger publishers and discounted books.

JB

I think it was already the same then though, and we were just lucky.

GE

There has been a shift in how bookshops see their audiences. When I started working in Waterstones, the people who worked there were buyers in charge of sections, and that gave you the opportunity to buy what you liked, but also to develop an audience, and a freedom to expect a completely different sort of audience to come in. Whereas now, centralisation means buying is aimed at a majority market and it anticipates that all readers are exactly the same.

JR

What I'm always interested in, and what this comes down to is the relationship between a Book Works book and a book by another publisher. That's why I always liked being at Frankfurt, and also commissioning work for spaces that weren't gallery spaces, such as all the exhibitions we did in libraries — that sort of a public space — which seems to open up a different way of reading something.

Again: Beginning 2

GE

Shall we have another go at the second beginning and say something about the exhibition? It was a show constructed partly out of looking at our archives and that became a show of commissions — showing what we have done by doing it. Actually, I wonder if we can just think of it as a show about distribution?

JR

It was a show about archives, and the title *Again, A Time Machine* was borne out of an idea of looking ahead, and using that play of time archives are based on which preserves the past for the future. And we used that process with our own events to create links between then and now. For example in the last event at The Showroom — *Confrontational Perspectives* — we used this image of the Guerrilla Girls from *Book Works, A Women's Perspective* … an exhibition and a conference we organised in 1992.[21]

PS

Is that image from the Book Works event?

JR

I'm not completely sure …

GE

It's an image from our archive with a note on the reverse saying 'COPYRIGHT / PLEASE CREDIT, BETH RIDGELL, DUBLIN, IRELAND', and a telephone number. Actually, it could be a press still.

JR

Well, they definitely took part in the panel discussion at *A Women's Perspective*, but I'm not sure if that image is from the conference. They are wearing masks so I can't tell you if that was the Guerrilla Girl who came or another one. And only myself and one other person saw them without theirs masks on.

KDF

Where was the exhibition held?

---

21 *Book Works, A Women's Perspective*, 1992, exhibition and conference with Sharon Kivland, Lily R Markiewicz, Deborah Levy / Sheila Burnett, Susan Johanknecht / Katharine Meynell, Adrian Piper, the Guerrilla Girls, Marysia Lewandowska, etc.

JR

The exhibition was in an old warehouse in Whitechapel and it explored some feminist issues. It had new work we commissioned and a collection of books from women artists like Kathy Acker, Sophie Calle, Jenny Holzer, Mary Kelly, Barbara Kruger and Adrian Piper, whose book *Colored People* was launched at the same time.

Dear Friend,
  I am black.
  I am sure you did not realize this when you made/laughed at/agreed with that racist remark. In the past, I have attempted to alert white people to my racial identity in advance. Unfortunately, this invariably causes them to react to me as pushy, manipulative, or socially inappropriate. Therefore, my policy is to assume that white people do not make these remarks, even when they believe there are no black people present, and to distribute this card when they do.
  I regret any discomfort my presence is causing you, just as I am sure you regret the discomfort your racism is causing me.
Sincerely yours,
Adrian Margaret Smith Piper

GE

What were the main issues of the conference? Do you remember the panel discussion with the Guerrilla Girls?

JR

It wasn't really a discussion. It was more a series of presentations. The Guerrilla Girls were talking to each other about their approach to the issues raised in their work; Adrian Piper talked about her work in relation to gender and race, Hilary Robinson gave a paper on Sophie Calle's *Suite Vénetienne*, the book project she did when she followed someone to Venice — so it was a 'reading' of Sophie Calle's work. I don't remember any panel discussions as such, unlike the conference for *Put About*, where groups of people discussed a particular topic.[22]

GE

So, it sounds similar to the performances that have occurred in *Again, A Time Machine*, say the revisited feminist event … have the issues shifted a lot?[23]

JR

Well, I think the issue then was whether artists' books were a genre in which women artists could work more successfully, because work could be produced on the kitchen table at home, on a small budget, so it was sort of to do with being a woman and the economies of scale. Although we organised it as an overview of what a group of women artists were doing, we didn't have any overriding political aims with it, or thought it was taking it anywhere. It wasn't that sort of conference. The term conference was probably wrong. Today it would be a series of talks and events. The only thing that made it conference-like was that it lasted two days, which you can't imagine now, and I think we made people pay thirty pounds for the two days. It was quite intense, as I remember.

JB

Was it just women?

JR

Pretty much, with one or two men in the audience. Unfortunately there's not much documentation of the conference itself.

KDF

No. There are only photos of the exhibition and the two black and white photographs of the Guerrilla Girls. There is no documentation of the audience. It's a shame that there isn't more of those early audiences.

JR

Documentation in the early days tended to focus on the final product and much less on the audience, or environment that we found ourselves in. And it was generated as a response to what the press wanted. Features and articles were starting to be written about us and the artists we worked with, and for this we would have produced images of the work itself, but not necessarily the process or audience that informed the work. Also it was possibly a response to funding issues. When we started to apply for funding, documentation of previous events was needed. And over the years that has changed quite a lot. We've become more conscious of our audience as well as the finished works: a case of how our distribution has grown and informed how we position ourselves maybe.

KDF

There are a number of similarities between *Again, A Time Machine* and previous exhibition projects like *The Reading Room* and *Library Relocations* …

---

22   *Put About: A Critical Anthology on Independent Publishing*, edited by Maria Fusco with Ian Hunt, and *Put About: A Symposium on Contemporary Independent Arts Publishing*, Tate Modern, Bankside, London, 2004.

23   *Confrontational Perspectives* with Marina Vishmidt, Claire Mahklouf Carter and Chicks on Speed, *Again, A Time Machine*, The Showroom, 2012.

JR

Yes, it is very similar particularly to *The Reading Room*, which occurred in three cities, with twelve artists, with a quick succession of openings and a number of talks at each one. The difference is that with that exhibition the commissioned artists really took the spotlight, and anything else occurred as part of those commissions, whereas with *Again, A Time Machine*, there has been an accumulation of effects. Commissions have been accompanied by talks, performances and events — or the archival project *Make the Living Look Dead* — on a more equal basis. And the work has snowballed, so while we originally conceived Jonathan Monk's *A Poster Project* to appear at each venue, Slavs and Tatars' riverbeds was intended to be very specific to Eastside Projects, in Birmingham, but then the work toured to Vienna, and reappeared in a different form in Sharjah. Similarly with the newspaper *79.89.09.*, which now exists in two editions and a Portuguese translation. Stewart's show at White Columns got taken on by SPACE in London. For me this is where things are really exciting, and being able to initiate something is the best we can do if it is a bigger-scale project. We can't tour big pieces of sculpture around the world, but we can give the artists a way of doing that by kick-starting an idea. Which is the same with the newspaper. That is different from *The Reading Room*, where they were much more site-specific. So the piece that Joseph Kosuth did at the Bodleian Library couldn't be recreated anywhere else, it was specific to the space and the Voltaire and John Locke collections. The reading of it had to be there. The book, we did alongside it, could be everywhere.[24]

And the same with *After the Freud Museum*, although perversely once the Tate bought it, they have shown it everywhere. But it was probably at its most effective when we did it first at the Freud Museum, because it was specific to that context.[25]

GE

There seems to be a shift in the time-based structure from those exhibitions and projects that happened after which the books followed, to this project. For example, some of the performances that have happened for Book Works in the past are reappearing. There is a sense that the exhibition has both generated and fed off itself. Sarah Pierce's exhibition at The Showroom is reusing material that has been generated and looking to future appropriation, and Laure's project seems to be constantly eating itself, both in terms of what she has contributed and the future book.[26]

JR
I agree.

Again: A Coda

GE

Did we begin to talk about the second beginning?

JB

Yes, although a bit by comparison. I think the thing is that like the books we do, we want the exhibition and work to speak for themselves.

GE

And this book. The book's also not going to explain what happened, or how it got pulled together. Or why some strangers are in it.[27]

JR

So have we covered everything?

JB

What about distribution? Again. You said you thought the exhibition might be thought of as about distribution as much as archive.

GE

I just meant they were linked. Jonathan's *A Poster Project* seems to do that — archive and distribute at the same time. As with Dora's work, the accumulation and loose indexing of stories, to be read out, dispersed and further accumulated, and, as Jane mentioned, the Slavs and Tatars project and newspaper.

JR

You sounded terribly earnest when you said that.

24   Joseph Kosuth, *Two Oxford Reading Rooms*, Book Works, London, 1994.
25   Susan Hiller, *After the Freud Museum*, Book Works, London, 1994.
26   Sarah Pierce, *Sketches of Universal History* and Laure Prouvost, *The Artist Book*, both forthcoming from Book Works, London, 2012–13.

27   This publication was conceived as a space to create new work, specific to the page. It neither documents nor explains the exhibition but offers readers an insight into the process of distribution and archiving that artists, writers and publishers are engaged with. Most of the contributors were drawn from the artists and writers commissioned during the exhibition. A few other artists, writers and organisations were asked to contribute specifically to the book: John Russell, and McKenzie Wark for engagements with the possibilities that writing and language offers for distributive art practice; and project spaces ranging from A Estante to X Marks the Bökship as organisations that operate in similar but distinct ways to Book Works were asked to answer the questions 'Why distribute?', 'Why archive?'. Offering no analysis or explanatory basis, the book operates as an alternative space to the exhibition, and offers a synchronic view of independent and self-publishing and the artists engaged with it.

GE

Maybe we should have a conversation about humour?

JR

Why?

GE

Because it's funnier than distribution?

JB

Don't you think that humour is an internal thing and that on the whole Book Works is viewed as a very serious and professional organisation. And the things that we put out into the world may be made with humour, but they are not humorous. The thing that people see from the outside is the seriousness of it.

GE

Yes, but … I think that there is something quite important about humour and the way in which Book Works works that is to do with a playfulness and a seriousness. Dora García has written a response that is related to that, about laughing at the wrong thing.

JB

But playfulness is different, isn't it. It's to do with a lightness.

GE

Obviously Book Works has a lightness of touch … Jane's not taking this seriously now.

JR

I'm lost … I've completely lost it. Maybe we should go back to distribution?

GE

Isn't it covered in the section in this book? Why distribute? Why archive? We've our own contribution.

JR

Yes, and I suppose most of the contributions look at distribution in a broad sense.

GE

Along with their accompanying footnotes. Do you think that project spaces need footnotes? I mean, do you think they take themselves more seriously now?

JB

What do you see as the role of humour?

GE

I think that there is a difference between what happens in the mainstream, in museums and galleries, and with curators, that is presented as quite serious, but that is actually tragically, farcically funny, and not that interesting.

JR

What? Because of the pomposity of it?

GE

Yes, and I was thinking again about the relationship between what happened at the *Womens' Perspective* conference and *Again, A Time Machine*, and the idea that books might be a space for women to make a certain type of work that wasn't available in the mainstream. As we've been talking about the expanded field in which we operate — publication in the broadest sense — it does seem that many of the issues are very similar. The Guerrilla Girls were talking about the glass ceiling and using printed material to playfully and provocatively denounce the mainstream. In Claire's piece there was a preoccupation with the invisible and the uncomfortable, with what's not allowed in the gallery, which bears comparison with those early performance works of Adrian Piper. Chicks on Speed seem to share similar concerns, including the role of fun and the anarchic, which again is probably not wanted in most galleries.

JR

The work of Inventory would be another earlier example of that sort of fun.[28]

JB

I think there is a confidence that comes with being able to use humour, to be silly, to be absurd, and to be able to see the absurdity of any of kind of situation.

GE

Well, it has found a home in and with artists' books for a long time, with Fluxus, and mail art, for example. It's founded on the relationship between seriousness and the joke.

Do You Feel Crushed?

subscribe to

INVENTORY
Losing   Finding   Collecting

A sporadical journal devoted to material culture and maverick thought

Inventory was set up as a collective enterprise by a group of writers, artists and theorists in 1995. The journal may be seen as an anti-hierarchical catalogue, a critical heterology, an interdisciplinary space from which to put forward a paradoxical philosophy which aims to present a sociology embracing the marginal and the everyday, the theoretical and the base. Establishing a dialogue with its readers whereby new constellations of thought and image come together, concretised in the material phenomena around us.

---

28   *Smash This Puny Existence*, Inventory poster project and street interventions, London and Glasgow, commissioned by Matthew Higgs for *Publish and Be Damned*, 1999.

SMASH THIS
PUNY EXISTENCE
DECAPIT
SMAS THIS
PUNY EXISTENCE
FABRICATE!

Actually, you don't really have to look much further than Stewart's *Index of Abandoned Material* to see this.

  PS
What's your favourite line from the book, then?

  GE
Get your Giant Pilot into Clunie Reid's Cockpit.[29]

  JR
Has this anything to do with distribution? Or have we finished? [30]

29 Stewart Home, *Blood Rites of the Bourgeoisie*, Book Works,
    2010.
30 In the way the first parts of this interview skirted around
    the archive, the exhibition and another partial history
    this section was meant to address distribution. Instead,
    the conversation briefly mentions a couple of relation-
    ships between the present exhibition and previous ones,
    before being side-tracked. I suppose the thing about
    being sidetracked and the joke is that it's not controlled,
    it has repercussions that are unknown, which is similar to
    the function that publishing, distribution and the archive
    has for us.

Essay commissioned after the event *Book Works: Pasts and Futures*, with Francesco Pedraglio at Spike Island, 20.9.11.

If there's been a way to build it, there'll be a way to destroy it

Ian Hunt

It is exciting and disturbing to see a city building site. Exciting, because the activity of destruction and construction interrupts the usual circulation of streets, and puts one set of workers visibly making something among the information workers in transit or at lunch. The stacked materials and mounds of clay, the exposed excavations glimpsed through the hoardings, and the new, unexpected vistas are deeply stimulating to the imagination. The experience is also disturbing, because it is frequently quite difficult mental work to recall what has been demolished, especially if you are in a part of the city you don't often walk through. Increasingly, I find I cannot remember what has been knocked down. There's a massive construction site opposite James Stirling's postmodern No. 1 Poultry, at the heart of the City of London. What has gone? North of Oxford Street, in Fitzrovia, there's another huge site. My brain had to work and work before I could recall anything of the visual features of the old dark red Middlesex Hospital. In every part of London there are political and economic processes at work that result in extraordinary physical and social effects. We should say what is happening as clearly as we can: that capitalism in its current form requires what Paul Connerton names as the repeated, intentional destruction of the built environment.

The effects are devastating for settled communities. Post-war housing estates north of Euston, which Frank Auerbach documented going up in a memorable series of paintings, are now threatened with destruction by the high-speed rail link.[1] However, there is a more obscure kind of shock at the process of intentional destruction, as you see that even quite bland parts of corporate London are not allowed to consolidate their own qualities. Between Liverpool Street station and Book Works' premises in Holywell Row lies the Broadgate development. The buildings are standard issue 1980s, the materials are flashy, and the shops and cafés are uninspiring (especially since Books etc. has closed — bookselling is rapidly withdrawing from city spaces). Nevertheless, as a piece of urban design, Broadgate works. From the transitional space around the Richard Serra sculpture, through the multi-level square with its Colosseum-like arena (which becomes an ice rink in winter — the seasons aren't banished) and on to the other squares and footways, this is a place not fully open to visual understanding. You have to explore it, and you cannot fully hold it together as a visual object. As a result there's a particular pleasure in passing through its successions of spaces.

Left:
Middlesex Hospital site from BT Tower, showing retained façade on Nassau Street and the chapel, designed in 1897 by John Loughborough Pearson.

1 Barnaby Wright, ed., *Frank Auerbach: London Building Sites 1952–1962*, Courtauld Institute Gallery, London, 2009.

35

Part of this development, too, is currently being demolished and redeveloped, after Jeremy Hunt blocked English Heritage's recommendation that it be listed at Grade II*. It is hard to imagine that something better will result. I saw it going up and now I see it coming down. This makes me feel, not so much a simple sense of time passing, as a deeper shock that the humanising and social qualities of even a semi-corporate place like Broadgate count for nothing, they are not acknowledged — apparently not seen or understood by developers intent on profit and ministers interfering in the planning process.

This lengthy preamble to a retrospect on Book Works' pasts and futures is in part a result of thinking about Paul Buck's 2011 Book Works publication, *A Public Intimacy (A Life Through Scrapbooks)*. Buck approaches the territory of life-writing through sharing his materials, allowing us to look over his shoulder at the cuttings he clipped from music papers, the pictures and scraps he thought to keep and organise as he constructed his life as a writer, editor and translator. The effect is intimate but also estranging and historical in an original way. Instead of concealing the process of filtering and sorting that any autobiography or retrospect depends on, we are allowed into it through the semi-public space of the scrapbook. Buck's unfinished projects and potential plans appear here with equal weight alongside what was achieved. The reader is actively engaged in what it means to construct a narrative of a life that opens outwards to a living sense of the time in which it unfolded. The effect is strangely bifocal: sometimes detail overwhelms you — there's a sense of the littlenesses that life is made from — but the book is also genuinely historical. Autobiographical claims to representativeness ('I, as a jazz fan, as a reader of French literature, as a moviegoer, speak for, exemplify …') rarely convince in this way. Buck also ensures that the social focus of the generational moment, which the psychoanalyst Christopher Bollas proposes as approximately the time one is in one's twenties and thirties, is allowed equal space and attention with the decades that follow it.[2]

Buck's writing and thinking in this book gave me an idea of how to gather the thoughts about place memory that I wanted, somehow, to interrupt and contextualise the invitation to look back on Book Works, especially in what I think of as its early period in the 1990s — though this was really a second period, after the time in three railway arches at Green Dragon Court, Borough Market (1984–92; I missed all the exhibitions held there and in the public spaces of the market). For it seems to me that, as an arts organisation as well as a publisher, Book Works has made a serious and creative connection with particular places, physically and socially. Place of publication is still part of the standard information any bibliography requires, and many kinds of history can be told through the scant evidence of publishers' addresses, but I mean something different from this. I mean that the history of Book Works can't be grasped simply from the printed record of the books themselves, substantial as that is. A different kind of history opens up if I start to sketch the way in which, from its beginnings and then through the 1990s, Book Works' exhibitions, launch parties, projects and events continued to be so responsive to the fascination of place. Each book was worked on with love and care. Each party had to be in the right place. The making of social events and celebrations that are truly special and memorable is a craft every bit as important as editing, design and printing.

I had first encountered Book Works as a bookseller. The three books published in 1990, by Pavel Büchler, Brian Catling and Verdi Yahooda, were not like books I had ever seen. Catling's *The Stumbling Block* was letterpress not as fine printing, but as physical definitiveness for extraordinary prose.[3] I made a display case for it in the bookshop where I worked and turned over a different page each day, as though it was a Christian Science Bible displayed to the street. Pavel Büchler's *Notable Days* masqueraded as a normal paperback while containing hardly any words, just an amazing feat of pictorial editing of half-tone news images of the revolution in Czechoslovakia (which had just happened). The price of the special edition was tied to the quoted price of 12 troy ounces of silver on the metal exchanges at the date of purchase. Verdi Yahooda's *Guidelines to the System* was bound in manila pattern-cutter's board, deeply embossed with a pattern in white. The loose-leaf photographs, held by metal fasteners, made reference to tailoring, which by this time was in transition, as dominance in the trade shifted from one immigrant group to another. A story by Craigie Horsfield, an enigmatic inclusion in the book, attempted to reconstruct an event in Kraków seventeen years previously. What conclusions might be drawn from these books, as a group? One was that London was Eastern Europe, among many other places: that it was radically strange, made by migrations, and still being made by them. Another was the strong concern with cultural memory. *The Stumbling Block* drew on contemporary London but also on history — of executions and coal mining, of anthropology and streets — from the nineteenth century and before, from history that still seemed alive to Catling. *Guidelines to the System* connected vividly and enigmatically with historical changes in work, craft and gender, at the intimate level of how bodies are clothed, how cloth is cut. The launch for these books, with installed works by Yahooda and Büchler, was held in a Spitalfields weaver's house rented by an up-and-coming tailor. The house was spellbinding: truly magical. The art Yahooda made for that occasion and that house honoured the past of the place in a real way. I had never been in such a place, apart from the Princelet Street Synagogue (at night, with the oral historian Alan Dien, who had a key). These places are special, but do not vanish because their specialness has been noticed. They still exist; they are obstacles to the usual flows of time, and are not stuck in a fleeting moment of fashion, interior decorating or journalistic attention.

This period of Book Works, the early 1990s, seems to me to be marked by an awareness of the paradoxes of pastness in relation to place: how the predatory set-dressing of the heritage industry — the term was only first coming into wide use in this period — was muddled up with the possibility of what a genuine short-circuiting of heritage clichés could be like. Artists were excited by this, and aware that their interest in the past and in historical recoveries was not innocent. It was an exciting moment because the radicality of responding to place as a worthwhile form of art-making had not yet become part of a curatorial routine. When I was first looking

2   Christopher Bollas, 'Generational Consciousness'
    in *Being a Character: Psychoanalysis and Self Experience*,
    Routledge, London, 1993.

3   *The Stumbling Block* has since been reprinted in its entirety
    in the *Oxford University Press Anthology of Twentieth-Century
    British and Irish Poetry*, ed. Keith Tuma, Oxford University
    Press, Oxford, 2001, and in Catling's collected poems, *A
    Court of Miracles*, Etruscan Books, Exbourne, 2009.

at art consistently in the 1980s, this way of working — site-specifically and in relation to place — seemed, like performance, to demonstrate and encourage a particular kind of resistance and awareness. The audiences for these works felt special, as though recruited to a worthwhile cause.

It is perhaps a separate point, but the artists Book Works worked with were also hard to place in terms of then current art. Some, like Catling, had been pretty much written off as strangers to the main flow of art history. At the same time there were collaborations with younger artists who would produce work of lasting interest, at a time when British art was beginning to resemble an overheated futures market. And there were international connections: with Adrian Piper and the Guerrilla Girls, who participated in *Book Works: A Women's Perspective* in 1992, with Jimmie Durham in 1993, and many others. These international links with the London base have of course continued. Book Works was prepared to collaborate with all these artists with a seriousness of commitment and care that enabled them to realise works of ambition and depth at a point in their progress when it mattered to be able to do so. The obvious local institutional parallels here are Matt's Gallery and Artangel, one strongly rooted, the other mobile. All these are important aspects of Book Works' history; but I want to return to its particular relation to place and cultural memory.

In 1994 an ambitious set of works was commissioned from artists and writers for a project called *The Reading Room*, held in several cities in England and Scotland. The idea was to explore the public place of books and reading: to investigate, as the booklet put it, 'how we "read" art, and what the future may bring in terms of our experience of reading'. Orthodox gallery spaces were used, along with libraries and other sites such as the Royal Botanic Garden in Edinburgh, and the Castle Mound, Oxford, which conceals a well in its interior chamber — at the time it was a neglected scruff of grass, the chamber rarely open; it is now part of a flourishing castle / prison quarter. Susan Hiller's work, conceived and commissioned for the Freud Museum in Maresfield Gardens, Hampstead, was one of the lasting and substantial results of *The Reading Room*, and has since become well known.

The use of such resonant sites for the Reading Room projects invited works that addressed issues of cultural memory. But the sense of 'pastness' that somehow attached itself to Book Works in this period was not invariably pursued by its chosen artists. Douglas Gordon, one of the younger artists commissioned, wrote in a diary of his project:

> July 1993. I make a first visit to look at various sites in Oxford; the Bodleian Library, Green College, the Ashmolean, the Radcliffe Camera and so on. I think Book Works want me to make an installation of text, something like something I might have done before; a critique on knowledge, power and the literary traditions of the city, I suppose. They haven't actually said this to me, it's just a feeling I get. I don't really want to do this.[4]

Gordon eventually decided 'not to tackle any literary or historical aspects of the city', half expecting (or hoping) that this could be a problem for Book Works. He chose a smallish, neutral gallery space, the Dolphin Gallery in St John's College, painted it all deep blue, and placed in it nothing but a simple sound system, which played pop songs he may or may not have heard while he was in his mother's womb, between January and September 1966. It was a reconfiguring of the idea of the reading room as an 'internal/aural space', and a conceptually witty response to thinking about the first possible encounters with what could be called received information. It was also a kind of generational statement in its perky avoidance of obvious signifiers of worthiness.

Gordon was free to make the work he wanted to make; but the orientation to cultural memory and the living presence of the past, which continued in some of the projects selected by Book Works in 1997 for libraries in London, Manchester and Liverpool (under the title *Library Relocations*), was nevertheless a positive strategy. Pamela Golden made a complex work for the British Architectural Library at RIBA, London: a printed edition on translucent paper, which was displayed on the top of the bookcases. It could only be viewed from a balcony, with opera glasses. There was a mass of source material and potential themes in this work, all overlaid on one another: the British Empire, medicine and health, the weather. I'll focus on just one: the system of memorisation known as the memory palace or the 'art of memory', which provided a structure for the work.

The memory palace is a mental building and a mnemonic device. Having visualised the building, with its rooms, windows, niches and portals, you then have a structure in which to place various objects or images that you may need to remember, for example when making a speech. According to Quintilian, in a text read by Pamela Golden as part of the video that introduced viewers to the work,

> This done, as soon as soon as the memory of the facts requires to be revived, all these places are visited in turn and the various deposits are demanded from their custodians, as the sight of each recalls the respective details. Consequently, however large the number of these which it is required to remember, all are linked one to the other like dancers hand in hand, and there can be no mistake since they join what precedes to what follows ...[5]

It was perhaps inevitable that at some point an artist Book Works commissioned would incorporate the art of memory into their work, as part of a widely shared underlying interest in cultural memory and archivalisation. But what fascinates me now, revisiting the memory palace idea, is that it features prominently as a counter-example in a persuasive and important account of forgetting, Paul Connerton's *How Modernity Forgets*. Connerton discusses the art of memory and notes how each memory is *located*. It is dependent on having a place. He proceeds to distinguish the memorial (a form bound up with an anxiety about what gets forgotten) from the *locus*, the locus being a more matter of fact and taken for granted part of our

4   Jane Rolo and Ian Hunt (eds.), *Book Works: A Partial History and Sourcebook*, Book Works, London, 1996, p.55.
5   Quoted from my essay on Golden's work in *Library Relocations*, Book Works, 1997.

daily experience. Paradigmatically, the locus takes the form of the house (itself a mnemonic device, that tells us each day how it is to be used, and what values it encodes) and the street.

> … we experience a locus *inattentively*, in a state of distraction. If we are aware of thinking of it at all, we think of it not so much as a set of objects which are available for us to look at or listen to, rather as something which is inconspicuously familiar to us. It is there for us to live in, to move about in, even while we in a sense ignore it. We accept it as a fact of life, a regular aspect of how things are.[6]

The larger connection that Connerton makes is between the explosion of interest in cultural memory that marked the end of the twentieth century and shows little sign of stopping, which he calls *hypermnesia* (too much remembering) and the structures of forgetting that are built into contemporary experience, the political economy, and the organisation of material processes. He analyses forgetting in terms of different temporalities: the time of the labour process, the time of consumption, the time of career structures, and the time of media and information production. He proceeds to examine the topographies of forgetting, and asks, 'what is the effect of the produced spaces of contemporary culture on the transmission of cultural memory?' The answer is that they generate 'a particular kind of cultural amnesia'. This thesis is explored with great patience and care by looking at three questions that affect deep assumptions about human settlement. 'The first is the scale of human settlement. The second is the production of speed. The third is the repeated, intentional destruction of the built environment.'[7]

It is only the third of these that I have been able to explore in this essay, as part of an account of a publisher, some of the artists and writers it has worked with, and the places it has worked in. Book Works' connections with place through books, exhibitions, events and celebrations are vital and imaginative. Cultural memory, which can't ultimately be separated from place, featured strongly as an underlying concern in early Book Works publications, and has continued to surface subsequently, in posters by Inventory, books by Luca Frei, Usman Saeed and Sukhdev Sandhu, Rosalind Nashashibi, Bridget Penney and Paul Buck, among others. But my point is not to bolster the case for a particular interpretation of Book Works' output. I want to look outward from publishing to some of the wider issues concerned. Connerton suggests that we seem to be caught in a paradox, in that we live in a culture of too much remembering, of hypermnesia, in which 'the radio, press and television are continually producing a chaotic reprise of a comprehensive archival deposit', and at the same time in a political economy that, among many other factors, repeatedly destroys the material experiences, the very ordinary and taken for granted qualities of streets and cities. This leads to the conclusion that we are also 'living in a post-mnemonic, a forgetful culture'. The paradox is resolvable 'once we see the causal relationship between these two features. Our world is hypermnesic in many of its cultural manifestations, and post-mnemonic in the structures of the political economy'.[8]

These are large questions, but Book Works is an unusual public interest company. Company histories are written by the victors. The histories of unusual companies can be a more open affair, and allow a view of the social contexts in which they function: those that are sustaining, and those that destroy.

6   Paul Connerton, *How Modernity Forgets*, Cambridge
    University Press, Cambridge, 2009, p. 34.
7   Ibid., p. 99.
8   Ibid., pp. 146–47.

WHAT HAS BEEN ONCE IS FOR ETERNITY
Slavs and Tatars

The *takht* (literally 'bed' or what we call 'river-bed' in honour of its ideal location by a source of water), the vernacular structure found at tea houses (*chai-khânehs*), roadside kiosks, shrines, entrances to mosques and restaurants across Iran and Central Asia, accommodates a group of roughly four or five people, without the unfortunate and unspoken delineation of individual space dictated by the chair. Friends, families, and colleagues sit, smoke shisheh, sip tea, eat lunch, take naps, and create a sense of public space, however momentarily, all the more remarkable in countries where public space is circumscribed, such as Iran.

In a span of a couple years, the *takht* has become the closest thing imaginable to a rider for Slavs and Tatars. Alas, no bathtubs filled with Borjomi spring water greet us in hotel rooms paid by public institutions, nor is fresh green tarragon disbursed with our per diems. As much as we would like to define the particular tastes of a Eurasian diva, we are grateful to the *takht* for allowing us and others — be it in Bukhara or Birmingham, Gent or Gdansk — a place to sit, talk, and read collectively.

Like a talisman of sorts, this seemingly simple three square metre wooden platform, has forced us to reflect on such elusive notions as generosity, participation, and pedagogy. How does one create a physical space for discourse without the prescriptive, precious and often exclusive trappings of art? Attempting a slippage or affinity of activities, we immediately grafted the act of reading onto the *takht*. After all, perhaps the only thing better in life than reading ... is reading while lying down, or reading while smoking, sipping tea, snacking, or napping. *For our Friendship of Nations: Polish Shi'ite Showbiz*, the *takht* served simultaneously as guide and locus to our investigation of the unlikely heritage between Poland and Iran from seventeenth-century Sarmatism to the twenty-first-century Green Movement. First commissioned by Book Works and Eastside Projects, *Dear 1979, Meet 1989* held an archive of books and printed matter on Poland's Solidarność and the Iranian Revolution. Seducing the public — from Baluchi labourers in need of a nap in Sharjah to Albanian bibliophiles in Thessaloniki — by the very primal need to sit down, this seating structure has allowed visitors different points of entry into otherwise rather complex subject matter. On various *rahlés*, book stands traditionally used for holy books such as the Qur'an, one could trace the story of two countries' attempts at self-determination via two major moments — 1979 and 1989 — that served as bookends to the major geopolitical narratives of the twenty-first and twentieth-centuries, political Islam and Communism, respectively.

Dervixe Qaderi do Kurdistão

O Metafísico
versus o Material

A Revolução Iraniana é a primeira e única revolução da era moderna a avançar uma agenda metafísica. As revoluções estão fadadas a falhar: como qualquer um que esteja remotamente familiarizado com as Revoluções Francesa ou Russa pode atestar. Uma coisa é cumprir certas promessas – não importa o quão elevadas, seja um governo do proletariado, a abolição da monarquia, etc.

e outra be
salvação, e
independe
Isso lev
bobagem
não se po

Qaderi Dervish do Kurdistão

Teocracia = Estado de D
República = Estado do
= Materialismo

A agitação recente no Irã, seguindo as eleições presidenciais de 2009, na verdade, pode ser atribuída às próprias origens e nome do país. O nome em si – a República Islâmica do Irã – são duas filosofias de governo divergentes e praticamente mutuamente excludentes: o estado de Deus encontrado em uma teocracia e o estado do homem encontrado na república. Somente depois que o trauma da guerra Irã – Iraque terminou e o país voltou a ter uma sensação de normalidade é que essa tensão veio à tona, inicialmente

com o gov
Hoje, a cli
República
Rafsanjani
republican
de contas
(president
Ayatollah
teocracia
prestação

9/2009

uma
do Shah
para
sição de
le Khomeini.
ncio de
Irã, como as

de 20.000 rial ou 2.000 toman e 50.000 rial ou 5.000 toman, o equivalente às notas de dois e cinco dólares americanos, respectivamente, são muitas vezes encontradas com slogans do protesto presidencial de 2009 escritas: 'Onde está meu voto?', 'Vida longa a Moussavi', 'Morte ao regime que engana o seu povo'

so) e slogan do movimento pró-Verde – Onde está meu voto? Vida longa a Moussavi!
ntemporânea (inscrições)

ГОР *бl*
ОТ
УМА

KIDNAP OVER-HERE

AND

MARRY OVER-HERE
OVER THERE

ƏSAS QAÇIRMAQDIR,
HARADA EVLƏNMƏYIN
FƏRQI YOXDUR

FOOL ME ONCE,
SHAME   ON   ARABIC.
FOOL ME TWICE,
SHAME   ON   CYRILLIC.
FOOL ME THRICE,
SHAME   ON   LATIN:
AaaaaaahhhhZERI!!!

دیگ د بوتی آو مونوگلوتس
بات ماری، مای چایلد، ای پولیگلوت

Диг да бути ов моноглотс
Бат марри, май чайлд, э полиглот

DIG THE BOOTY OF MONOGLOTS
BUT MARRY, MY CHILD, A POLYGLOT

Commissioned for *Again, A Time Machine* exhibition, artist's talk and newspaper publication *79.89.09.*, Eastside Projects, 26.2.11 to 16.4.11; Spike Island 16.9.11 to 9.10.11; and *What has been once is for eternity*, for *Again, A Time Machine* publication, 2012.

Pages 42–43: Omon-Xona, near Boysun, Uzbekistan.

Page 44: Ali, the invigilator, at the 10th Sharjah Biennial, 2011, photograph by Elizabeth Rappaport.

Page 45: prayers at the tomb of Bahaud'din Naqshband, outside Bukhara, Uzbekistan.

Page 46: *Przyjazn Narodów: Lahestan Nesfeh-Jahan* at GGM, Gdansk, Poland. Insert, stone *rahlé* in Bibi Khanum's mosque in Samarqand.

Page 47: detail from *79.89.09.* (Portuguese edition), 2011.

Pages 48–49: *Friendship of Nations: Polish Shi'ite Showbiz*, Kiosk Gallery, Gent, Belgium, photograph by Yana Foque. Insert, *Friendship of Nations: Polish Shi'ite Showbiz* (installation view,), 10th Sharjah Biennial, Sharjah, UAE. Photograph by Alfred Rubio / Sharjah Art Foundation.

Pages 50–51: *takht* in a restaurant with winter cover and heated floors, Torghabeh, Iran. Insert top, courtyard of Tabatabai house in Kashan, Iran. Insert below, shrine of Khwaja Mahmoud al-Anjir al-Faghnawi outside Bukhara, Omon-Xona, Antica Hotel, Samarqand.

Pages 52–53: dikkat of Sultan Ahmed Mosque, Istanbul. Insert, *Moslems of the Soviet Union* in English and Arabic.

Pages 54–55: Detail from back page of *79.89.09.* Insert, *PrayWay*, 390 x 280 x 50 cm, wool carpet, steel, MDF, neon, *The Ungovernables*, New Museum of Contemporary Art, New York, 2012.

Graded at number six

Apexa Patel

1   *I always attempt to begin at the perigee of a strange object covered in fur which breaks your heart,* in the hope that I can maintain a steady course without slipping too easily into the unfavourable section, where now amongst the shortcomings of your vocabulary, you must also sit with people who have been using the word existential far too much. Somehow, I know that this will feel even worse than the oppo-site** of where I was hoping to be, so I quietly rely on everyone's generosity in developing amnesia when needed, in other words, I apologise in advance.*

2   *   I have gone from losing hours in awkward proximity, forgiving shallow intentions because the consequences are such to being at the bar with what feels like a statistically unlikely number of people, all of whom keep putting their hand on their heart before saying *poignant*. All I ever wanted was a slight consensus over the rare condition of experience outweighing language, this must obviously be my punishment. How is it that a word that derives from the French word *poindre* or a Latin word I cannot pronounce, meaning to prick or sting and possibly even punch has gone on to become a stand-in for a little bit of whimsy? Surely only a few things in the world elicit such a visceral response?

3   The question has prompted the arrival of the inevitable point in the evening, where I start displaying the verbal skills of a foreigner whose English even at its best, is not quite resembling Globish. I imagine they were expecting some kind of introduction, followed shortly by flawless rhetoric, and what they got instead was my impression of someone suffering from generalised anxiety disorder. I compose myself and try to illustrate my point by recounting the story of a friend whose forty-five minute, near silent critique forced him to question whether destroying conversation can be seen as the success of years of hard work or the absolute failure. I proposed that any situation in which people have stopped speculating about what the lowest common denominator is could not be a source of disillusionment, as it is useful to think of all the terrible art Walter Benjamin is inadvertently responsible for.

     In trying to hold on to whatever clarity I have left, I scan every potential strategy I have assigned myself trying to find the most appropriate focus and synchronisation, which is basically a futile exercise in pleasing everyone you have ever loved whilst knowing that theft is not the way forward.

1   Barthelme.
2   Warhol.
3   Hickey.

4 The obvious option appears frequently with minimal elaboration. It is obscure, generous and endlessly inventive in ways that are difficult to articulate, especially once you have assimilated someone else's insightful analogy about an unwanted seat mate on a bus journey, who over a subtle conversation arc, proves to you that you know far less than you had initially thought. Unfortunately on this occasion, the vernacular is letting me down, meaningful translation is vaporising and there are too many pejorative clichés that have been put into circulation thus preventing an explanation in how the question of *who do you have continuity with?* might work when playing badminton.

5 I am made to be very aware of the inherent formalism that is present in talk value and how it is about to combine with my inability to recognise when I have crossed the boundary of taste, by that I mean, I no longer know what constitutes good design in this case. It would seem that my temporary resolve of ignoring a credible body of work on the notion of kitsch is on the brink of extinction. So I seriously start to think that the gathering under the tree is in urgent need of a cool, contemporary makeover. In the meantime, I keep looking to these lists to learn the rules as if manifestos were maps but I am no better acquainted with the information. I actually feel like I am projecting something in the vicinity of the dumbest, smartest design equation, where you deal with the intricacy of proposing a solution even when there is no problem.

6 This is not too far off from a fear of the highly probable scenario in which a rather astute counter argument eclipses your view; kind of what the powerhouse intellectual did to the minor legend or what the minor legend did to the powerhouse intellectual depending on what you subscribe to.

   What I assume is actually happening is that there is a dynamic contradiction that is at play, where through sheer will and luck, you are able to identify a vast array of gaps in one's general understanding but once you are in the position to expand on these discrepancies, you stand back and do not do what seems to be the logical thing to do, as a result of estimating that it will be characterised by the application of an annoying mirror reflection device. I do not think it is a mistake that this paradox is also apparently called aprofound.

   In light of there being no compelling evidence, I wonder who carries the burden. Everyone acknowledges an appearance of what is being done here, function on the other hand is obtuse. I for my part, am being looked at in the sort of way that would suggest, *I understand your vacillation, I do not care for its aesthetic though I will tolerate its structure in order to learn of the case that I think you are privately cultivating.*

7 It would seem that I am not the only one waiting for these ideas to be presented in radically attenuated form. They exist as such, alongside erudite, deeply layered and rhizomic prospects. They are interesting as far as the paraphrase, after which it becomes an uphill battle. I am somewhat sceptical about this practice ever becoming my property as I am still very much in the process of having to negotiate the meaning of every singular word, with which the options

of definition consist of more than two choices and the available context has ceased to help in providing a vague outcome.

There is also the rather frustrating employment of three words or variations on the theme of numerous words when it would just be much simpler to have one, monolithic stance of total dismissal. This ought to produce polarity and a degree of conflicting positions, but ideas diverge and inflate in different dimensions, generating their own distinguishable environments in which no one is laughing whilst decomposing an expression.

I am advised to suspend at the beginning, but I leave it till the end, if there is a significant other side, it is in a curious state.

8   **   To compensate for this tedious realisation, I indulge in the easier alternative of marking out the negative space in which there is an exciting moment earlier, where everyone has this frantic search for the most attractive person in the room. Now, I stare at this guy to see if these strategies work, he has smiled, so I am thinking, no?

My attempts of embracing the current ethos have failed. I have been lying across the floor in all kinds of embarrassing positions trying to access complexity from every angle, much in the spirit of the in and outy dance that is performed before painting. Yet even then, the only art I manage to grasp is this beautifully sequined and beaded, white dress that, looking at the size of the person wearing it, could totally be the right cut for me. It is not surprising to discover, that minutes later where I have casually given up on the ritualistic gestures that I must abide by in a queue, that I can feel a whole line of people carefully disqualifying me from highbrow culture. The thing to remember at this point is that it is actually a very short distance from the disco dancer to M.I.A.

What is becoming increasingly apparent is that the success of this endurance depends entirely on whether you think of it as a spiritual retreat with offers of abstract rehabilitation. Consider for example, how long can you go without gravitating towards the Rich Tea biscuits and dried apricots? We have all been standing here trying to eat this weird combination of food at the kind of sluggish pace that in normal circumstances would be unimaginable. Somehow sipping water for several minutes does not provide immunity from the fact that once the supplies run out, you must finally confront the hours of boredom that you have signed up for all in the name of knowing what you are rejecting.

In my top two things I love about being here, is this slow walk. It is not only an excellent time killer but I am convinced that it must be viewed as choreography in some circles.

Those who were policing the situation have left. What I really wanted to know was, the scheduling of the segment that is going to allow me to practise my scream. But I still have my phone in my pocket, I do not have the notepad that was promised and most importantly, why am I allowed to leave whenever I want?

4   Gulzar.
5   Sheikh.
6   Gillick.
7   Barthes and Deleuze.
8   Abramović.

turned away from the library because I lacked a permit to examine the volume. Having no more than riffled through the pages before the librarian snatched it back, I had only the faintest idea what it was all about. But the title I had spotted in the catalogue - *My Book, The East London Coelacanth...* had been enough to fire my imagination. Its photographs of the author, gravely contemplating the canals into which he dangled his fishing line, dovetailed neatly with images of the large, blue, pelagic fish whose discovery was my goal.

Of course I had no idea of Durham's true motives in writing the book but there was something extraordinarily unsettling about his intervention. If he, like myself, was after the reward offered by Professor Smith for the capture of a second coelacanth then he would hardly have put down anything that would be of practical use in my quest... I dismissed the idea that Smith knew of the work. *He* wasn't obsessed with making his way through all the literature on the subject; penned as it was mostly by those who were only too ready to dismiss the idea of the coelacanth being a true Lazarus taxon... How, they argued, could a fish nearly five foot long have existed through eighty million years without leaving any trace of its presence? I considered the other creatures - unicorns, dragons, even mermaids - that wandered in and out of imagination but the coelacanth wasn't like them. *It* hadn't originated as a traveler's brag or developed independent life from a botched attempt to explain a mysterious body part...There was hard, scientific proof of its existence. The fish had been caught in a trawler's net at the mouth of the Chalumna river on Christmas Eve 1938 and identified as an unusual specimen by Marjorie Courtney-Latimer, curator of the East London museum, who had got in touch with Smith. It had been drawn, photographed, stuffed, mounted and was on display. The only problem – and the reason why Smith was so desperate to get his hands on a second specimen – was that the taxidermist had disposed of the soft tissues & guts of the fish before the professor had been able to examine them.

Though I was almost sure it was a red herring, I couldn't get Durham's book out of my head. The coelacanth's life-cycle was so mysterious that ruling anything out could be unwise. After all, Agassiz had conjured the name meaning 'hollow spine' from a fossil tail discovered while blasting out a road in northern England a century ago... When that fish had been alive all the continents had existed in a totally different configuration. In the same way populations of land animals had become isolated from each other when continents drifted, wouldn't fish have been separated when ocean channels closed up? In which case Durham's quest for its descendants in the waterways of the British metropolis rather than in the Indian ocean might not be as quixotic as it first appeared. Maybe, although his preoccupation with homonyms seemed odd, he was onto something... During the long voyage north in the ship's hold I studied the crumpled reward notice for the coelacanth I had ripped from the East London dockside and mused on Smith's theory that 'old fourlegs' might actually walk on the seabed. If the crossed extensor pattern of its fins offered a clue to how creatures had first come out of the sea onto the land was it a collateral ancestor of all the people looking for it?

Once in London, I slipped undetected from my ship and headed up Limehouse Cut. Regent's Canal wasn't promising but, though shallow and restricted by mechanical locks, water had to flow through it...and patience, while fishing, is essential. Since this incredible fish had persisted unchanged through aeons surely *I* could wait. I was staring over the concrete towpath, trying to backtrack my thoughts somewhere more useful, when the revelation hit me. Surely you would only stop evolving if perfection had been attained, and though that might be hard to define; on the other hand, since the East London specimen's vital organs were missing, not even the Professor had been able to make a guess at how old it was. It might be a Methuselah...then for a minute I couldn't breathe. Was it possible this large blue pelagic fish held the secret of eternal life? It would explain the absence of specimens younger than sixty five million years from the fossil record and in that case Durham was after bigger game than Smith's reward. Like a medieval alchemist he was

The Garboldisham Road:
sports commentary, scores and scripts

Melissa Gronlund

The archive was a principle issue of concern to art of the twentieth century, and, perhaps because of its demi-historical, demi-aesthetic nature, continues to exert a hold on theorists, artists and curators. The archive offered a reflective model for an art world struggling with its loss of aesthetic criteria, while World Wars I and II, the Cold War and the unfolding histories of post-colonialism offered history new, unassimilable events at the very moment that methodologies of history-writing were being conceptually undermined. More recently, this intersection between artistic interest in the archive and related problems in historiography reveal a move away from documentation and towards, instead, a space of actualisation, particularly in works that use the score — that Fluxus beast — to navigate between strict categories of 'document' and 'fiction'.

In the introduction to his forthcoming book on the archive, *Under Suspicion: A Phenomenology of Media*, Boris Groys argues that the effect of the archive as a repository is to create two spaces for historical artefacts: the 'sacral' — those effects that have entered into the eternal space of the archive — and the 'profane', those effects outside it. Those within the archive are to be saved for eternity, that is, and those without it are left to disappear. As such, the archive cannot represent what marks reality most insistently: its mortality. Moreover, the archive's insatiable demand for completion — its attempt to represent a total history — means that it grows and grows, continually absorbing within it the documents, items and paraphernalia that form a composite picture of the archived subject. As this sacral space increases, Groys writes, 'reality itself [becomes] secondary in relation to the archive: it is all that which has been left outside of the archive'.[1]

In this schema, Groys further posits a third category to be introduced into his couplet of 'sacral' and 'profane': this is the 'sub-medial' space that reminds the viewer, as in some primal scene, of the medial nature of the thing archived:

> At first glance, the sign carriers of the archive are topographically located within the archival space — like books in a library, canvases in a picture gallery or video-gadgets and computers in a video-installation. But this impression is deceptive.

1   Boris Groys, *Under Suspicion: A Phenomenology of New Media*, Columbia University Press, New York, 2012. Introduction available here: http://archivepublic.wordpress.com/texts/boris-groys

Books are not part of the archive, but texts are; not canvases, but paintings; not video-gadgets, but moving images. The carriers of the archive do not belong to the archive, because they remain hidden behind the medial surface of signs they offer to the observer of the archive. Or, put differently: the carrier of the archive does not belong to the archive, because although it sustains archival signs, it is not an archival sign itself. Much like the profane space, the carrier of the archive constitutes the outside of the archive.[2]

In creating this 'sub-medial' space, Groys attempts to reposition the philosophical question of ontology — its search for essence — within a world understood as one of signs, where essence can be read as non-sign, non-medial. However, this non-medial access is foreclosed to us — who can see a painting that's not made of paint and on canvas? — therefore, the search in media-ontology has to be read differently: 'the observer of the medial surface waits for the medium to become the message, for the carrier to become the sign.' In other words, how can we access the carrier of the painting itself, and read into that the infinitude of the archive?

This flickering back and forth between carrier and sign was anticipated in Siegfried Kracauer's early essay on photography ('On Photography', 1927), in which he suggested that photography would work to impede memory rather than enhance it. Contrary to the view that the photograph's indexicality — the fact that its chemical basis gives a truth-value to the contents it shows, as subjects must have been in front of a camera in order to be captured on celluloid — makes it a privileged vehicle for memory, Kracauer writes how the sheer number of photographs and remnants of the past overwhelm the individual's ability to understand and synthesise the information they contain. Not having any direct relation to it, one would simply make fun of the outmoded hairstyles or clothing seen in old photographs; the world, Kracauer writes memorably, becomes a blizzard of images, and the 'flood of photographs sweeps away the dams of memory'.[3] This sense of being engulfed, this inability to make sense of all the documents that the technologies of mechanical reproduction have now made available to us, is manifest in the number of works made in the twentieth century that use the archive as a historical model: Richter's *Atlas* (1962– present), Hanne Darboven's *Kulturgeschichte 1880–1983* (1980–83), for example, or the many monuments and installations of Thomas Hirschhorn's practice. These seek to re-create the archive spatially, employing vast amounts of material to phenomenologically evoke the sensation of being in a blizzard of the past, in which, despite and because of the vast amount of information maintained in the archive's sacral space, the archive emerges as an ambiguously successful tool of remembrance.

If the archive has been an unreliable watchman of history, traditional historiography has not fared much better. The annals of medieval history were — in a way the Conceptualists might appreciate — simply lists of the years, with details added if something interesting happened:

709. Hard winter. Duke Gottfried died.

710. Hard year and deficient in crops.

711.

712. Flood everywhere.

713.

714. Pippin, mayor of the palace, died.

715.

716.

717.

718. Charles devastated the Saxon with great destruction.[4]

Historiography was refined during the Renaissance, particularly in Italy, when humanist scholars looked to Greco-Roman models for writing history, and used these to glorify their state and its exploits. It was in many ways an unashamedly subjective version of history, written by the winners. The modern tradition of historiography is understood to have been fathered by Leopold van Ranke, a German historian of the 1800s, whose famous dictum was to write history 'wie es eigentlich gewesen' — as near as possible to how it actually was. This meant that the problems of historiography became problems of content, or put otherwise, memory: of not having enough accurate and trustworthy material from which to compile a perfect history of the event. The advent of reproductive technologies in the twentieth century, obviously, offered a tantalising solution to this problem. Arthur Danto writes that the ultimate historian, the 'ideal chronicler', would be the film camera: able to record the world as it is happening with no editorial or human intervention. But that boon of film, he continues, would be unwatchable: one needs to synthesise the material, to make some kind of story out of it, or else — like Kracauer's blizzard and Darboven's archive — it is non-sensical. This synthesisation poses its own problems, for at the same time that recording technology was becoming available, narratologists were arguing that historiography as presently written perverted the material, using it to tell a unified story rather than representing the messy, unaccountable business of historical facts. In what Hayden White has called the 'embarrassment of plot to historical narrative',historiography in the twentieth century grappled with the false sense of meaning that the writing of history as story leant to it.[5]

Hollis Frampton wrote a horror story of sorts where he imagined an heiress whose entire life has been filmed — a proviso of her 'loving and eccentric father'.[6] She has an extremely interesting life, survives all her children, and as her last bequest leaves her fortune to the first child born after her death in the same city in which she dies, on the condition that

2   Ibid.
3   Siegfried Kracauer, 'Photography', *The Mass Ornament*, Harvard University Press, Cambridge, 1995.
4   Quoted from Hayden White, *The Content of the Form: Narrative Discourse and Historical Representation*, Johns Hopkins University Press, Baltimore and London, 1990, pp. 6–7.

5   Ibid., p. 22.
6   Hollis Frampton, 'A Pentagram for Conjuring the Narrative', in Bruce Jenkins, ed., *On the Camera Arts and Consecutive Matters: The Writings of Hollis Frampton*, MIT Press, Cambridge, MA, 2009, p. 140.

the child spends his or her whole life watching the films of the woman's life. When the last reel ends, Frampton writes, the man chosen to fulfil her request, his life having passed in the watching of another's, his muscles atrophied, goes to sleep, unaware that he has watched the last reel, and dies. The story speaks to the narcissism allowed and even enabled by film — but also to the link between photography and death, which has popular echoes in the reported belief when photography was first encountered that taking a picture would steal your soul. Frampton, perhaps underscoring the witch-like nature of photography, presents this story embedded within the text 'A Pentagram for Conjuring the Narrative'. Kracauer, too, underscores the connection between death and photography, arguing that one takes pictures in order to stave off the idea that one might die one day: 'That the world devours them is a sign of the *fear of death*. What the photographs by their sheer accumulation attempt to banish is the recollection of death, which is part and parcel of every memory image.'[7] But for Frampton the camera and film apparatus are also elements of seduction: he presents a scenario in which photographs (or memory or history or the archive) are so highly prized, so real and lifelike, that they offer the temptation of taking the place of real life. Put differently, in its attempt to 'be' reality, the sacral space of the photograph rises above the plane of its pretended subject.

In his work *Situation Leading to a Story* (2000) Matthew Buckingham describes four reels of 16mm film he found on the street one night when returning home from a cinema in New York City. The film is comprised on these four reels, overlaid with his commentary of how he tried to trace the owner of the films, and what he speculated might connect them, one of which shows a wealthy family at home in upstate New York; another of the same house, though later; and the last two of miners in Peru. The 'story' of the film's title is Buckingham's story of finding the films and the 'situation' is the problem of uncontextualised pieces of information — if the word 'situation' doesn't feel right in the title, and to me it never has, it speaks to the unusualness of this set of circumstances. History left in its raw state does not have a name. This is apparent even on the micro level of the people in the home movies who are aware they are acting for posterity, for history, for the archive, but are not sure what they are meant to be doing: watching the people move across the lawn, perform leisure activities and smile at the camera shows, as Buckingham says, 'the familiar awkwardness of people performing their identity for a story without a plot'. Home movies aim to show us living our normal lives for the sole purpose of recording them. When we smile or introduce our room on camera, we are doing so in order to enter our lives into the sacral space of the archive — it is not a 'real' activity as such, but a futurospective one, something performed only for future gain. Whether this is still the case now that the world has *really* taken on a photographic face, to invoke Kracauer once more, when we have become so used to capturing things on camera that we have shifted to thinking of recorded images as a means of instant communication, rather than with a memorialising function of the future past, is germane to the question of the archive and to this Book Works' series, with its own haphazard logic of archiving. This text, for example, appeared first as a talk, in collaboration with Paul Buck and Sarah Pierce, who based its format on transcripts of previous Book Works talks, while Buck intervened and improvised on and with material from his own archive. This talk was recorded and exists somewhere in the Book Works office archive (and perhaps also in that of The Showroom, where it was held). One gets the sense that we are navigating the means of recording history by all means at once, as who knows what will stick, or how the past will manage to reappear.

Buckingham's film, with its addition of linguistic commentary, is concerned to show what the image lacks, and he uses his happenstance discovery of these unidentified reels as a pretext to show how much the image — any image — hides. Watching the silent footage of the construction of mines in Peru, for example, he discusses the history of US agribusiness in the country from the late 1800s onwards, and their domination of the natural resources in the country even after the mines were nationalised in the 1970s — histories that an image itself would not be able to communicate, and whose addition here transforms the images from personal travelogues into historical documents.

The muteness and adaptability of the photographic image have likewise been apparent since the beginning of the medium, from Benjamin's famous query about captions in 'A Little History of Photography' ('Will the caption become more important than the photograph?') to the Kuleshov experiment, which was instrumental to Sergei Eisenstein in his theory of montage. (Kuleshov, a psychologist, showed how subjects' interpretation of an image's meaning changes based on what the image is paired with. He interspersed into footage of the unchanging, blank face of a Soviet heartthrob of the day various images, such as a plate of food, a baby and a corpse, and asked viewers to rate how the man felt. After the plate of food, they said he felt hungry; after the baby, happy; and after the corpse, sad.) Benjamin, in particular, talked about the loss effected on images by an inability to read them pictorially (an 'illiteracy … of photography'), which resulted in the need to supplement images with captions.[8] This idea of a loss has perhaps been sidelined by the idea of the free radicality of the uncontextualised image, which has been the assumption of so much thinking about the archive, from Richter to Hirshhorn to Jacques Derrida. But it is closer to how one views an image in everyday experience, when one reads it as efficiently as possible in order to quickly glean information, allowing it to stand as mere illustration of the text.

But is there an alternative to this means of reading that results in this loss of pictorial information? Or is there commentary in which image and text are equal — in which the textual commentary is subordinate to, rather than determinate of, the image it accompanies? At this stage in the first manifestation of this text, the talk, and in a shameless bid to win over the audience, I played two YouTube clips to test these questions, which now reappear in ways that Pierce, Buck and I could not have anticipated — writing about writing that attempts to be less than images that are absent.

7   Kracauer, op. cit., p.59.
8   Walter Benjamin 'A Small History of Photography',
    in *One-Way Street and Other Writings*, New Left Books,
    London, 1979.

The first was from the recent wedding of Kate Middleton and Prince William, which I had watched on TV during the national holiday given over to this event. There was a lot of waiting for anything to happen as the TV networks had filmed from the arrival of the first guests — meaning for a few hours the TV audience was simply watching, or waiting, for dignitaries to file in. While this footage was happening, from time to time the commentators felt duty-bound to say something, but as there was nothing to say they simply repeated the visual information that was seen on screen — which, of course, the viewer could see too. As one of the cars carrying members of the royal family passed under an arch, a BBC commentator noted that the car had passed under an arch. Immediately one's attention swung to the arch. So, there was an arch. When Kate Middleton arrived, the commentator noted that 'you can see her dress, you can see her flowers', which were, indeed, visible. Even though I chose this clip because I remembered being struck by the tautological character of the commentary, while watching it again I realised that the spoken description of the scene did come to supersede the given visual information: so, I noticed her dress, and the flowers, and the make-up concurrently with the instruction, whereas if it were a silent film I might have noticed the car, the driver, or the ugly marquee she walked underneath instead.

So, I forced the audience into watching yet more images of Kate Middleton while explaining helpfully that despite the clip's apparent tautological structure, its commentary remained the over-determinate factor in the images' production of signification.

The second clip was even more unabashed. I was trying to think, again, of this possible parity between word and moving image, or where word is subordinate to image, and places where it might exist. So, I thought of sports commentary for radio, which is charged with re-creating a visual event for listeners at home, and aims to represent as fully as possible the visual field before it. To pare this down even further, I thought of the most boring sport I could, and searched for cricket commentary.

I found a wonderful and hilarious sketch by Stephen Fry and Hugh Laurie in which the two comedians play cricket presenters.[9] As is usual with cricket commentary, Fry and Laurie discuss what is going on around the players in the field — where there is much more going on — rather than the match itself: 'Oh look, there's a bus! There are people getting off the bus! The bus is going down the Garboldisham Road …' The sketch ends in a paroxysm of ecstasy for cricket and other joys of good-old-England. Words run away with themselves, and rather than subordinating their commentary to the events around them, their commentary ends up controlling them, to a farcical, exaggerated, eruptive extreme.

I am not sure if these two clips amount to a sustained argument of the tyranny of word over image, or its relentless drive to reduce visual information to only whatever is commented on, and I suspect that they do not. This text, moreover, falls prey to the very problem in this re-creation of the live, visual moment, in textual documentation. But I maintain that the exercise is instructive in both showing what is lost in contextualisation — the car, the driver, the marquee — and in its demonstration of the ease with which questions of representation and belonging emerge in the spoken voice behind the text, in the 'I' who writes. The interrogation of national, gendered or racial identities has been a key facet of the archive as an artistic methodology both in and outside areas of North America and Western Europe, which have, again, used the archive to activate the image's uncontextualised potential as well as its intimate linkage to the political. The archival techniques of Susan Hiller, Christian Boltanski, or Renée Green, for example, are joined by a number of archival projects launched in South America, the Middle East and Eastern Europe precisely because the archive as a tool allows for the recombination and, in its collecting material of everyday reality, of real contestation of accepted history. Beyond any theoretical ruminations of the aporia of archival form or medium, and its ability to overwhelm the present with the weight of history, the real strength of the archive as a tool lies in these practical exercises with the archive.

Here the great threat of the archive is also its great possibility: the reduction of different items to exchangeable signs. Eduardo Molinari of the Buenos Aires-based Archivo Caminante, or Walking Archive, calls this 'semiocapitalism', a term he borrows from Franco Berardi, where the recombination of signs is more important than the content they contain.[10] The different boxes of the Archivo Caminante, whose contents are free to consult and which reappear in different instantiations in different exhibitions, contain evidence and images that range from the photographs from Argentina's dictatorship, evidence of current agribusiness activity in Argentina, symbols of theory (for example, images of the huge head of Marx in Chemnitz, Germany), Incan objects whose functions are now barely remembered. Archivo Caminante actively fight against the consequences of profanity — the fact that the histories of objects do die — and faced with this reality of recuperating that which is no longer wholly present, uses this sign of art, which he operates under, to bring both 'real' and fiction into his constellations of 'truth' in the present.

In verging towards fictionality, Archivo Caminante and others move out of the idea of the archive as it has been properly defined. The liminal and temporally undefined space they inhabit — between demonstration and execution, instruction and existence — is more accurately that of the score or script. We might posit this form of art making, almost dialectically, as the riposte to the archive and the archive's hold on the twentieth century's imagination: text that does not refer backwards but which looks forward, whose completion lies in performance, leaving it — the text — in a state of always becoming that is, of course, near to archive's own quest for full and impossible completion.

* * *

9   See http://www.youtube.com/watch?v=G4ZgecMx9uI
10 Interview between Eduardo Molinari and Nancy Garín,
    1 October 2010, http://www.latinart.com/transcript.
    cfm?id=109.

The script is a descendant of Fluxus and Conceptualist instruction pieces and the confusion they generated of where the work resided: in the set of instructions or in the action they called for.[11] This ambiguity still lingers, positioning the script piece between document for performance and text piece. I would argue that the script has become a particular subject of attention over the past few years, partially due to an abiding Conceptualist interest in different notation schema (musical notation, architectural drawings, library decimal systems, etc.) and partially because the script occupies the place of the *à avenir* — the space of pure potential, where everything is still possible.

This potential for non-fixedness and near fictionality is marshalled within score works. Janice Kerbel's *Ballgame*, 2008– ongoing, is a multi-part project that represents the average baseball game in different media — a radio broadcast, score sheets. Kerbel constructed the game out of the average possibility that would happen at every moment in a ballgame — the average hit the batter would get at that average point in the average game, which would be followed by this average event etc. — mocking baseball's obsession with statistics but also enabling the game to be written of itself, without Kerbel's authorial direction. It was first exhibited (*Inning 1*) in 2008 as a spoken piece at Art Sheffield 08, again as an extract for Book Works' *Existential Territories* series in 2009, and later that same year (*Innings 1–3*) as a sound piece at Greengrassi, Kerbel's London gallery. A version of the script was also published in the magazine *FR David*. The relationship between score and the game it describes is deliberately ambiguous: on the one hand the typewritten score is the game, while on the other hand it is merely an evocation or a representation of the perfect average which Kerbel aims to create. Kerbel explains, 'Since it is written in "real time", it must be performed in real time to mimic the playing of the game. It must take 2 hours and 33 min (the average length of a game). There is a lot of "blank" space built into the edit. Since it is recorded with no ambient sound (crowd cheering, advertising etc.), I have used typographical notation to indicate this.'[12] The score both *is* and *must* take 2 hours and 33 minutes; moreover, it is written, as Kerbel says in quotation marks, in 'real time', suggesting that rather than being a document of the game,

the score, like the game itself, is in an eternal present of unfolding. And despite its apparent documentary (retrospective) status — occupying forms of commentary such as the score-sheet, script and the radio commentary, which generally follow rather than pre-date the event, the *Ballgame* exists within the temporal logic of performance in that only its live actualisation, through listening or reading, fulfils the active requirement that the text creates itself.

A similar confusion of temporalities is at play within Pablo Bronstein's score works. In his performance *The Birth of Venus*, 2011, at the ICA, London, Bronstein worked with dance notations from a series of prints to re-stage a Baroque ballet from 1636. To construct the dance Bronstein and his collaborators used surviving notation devices from that period of the dancers' movement on the floor.[13] Using the floor designs as a lost language for performance, as when philologists guess at pronunciation of dead languages from their rhymes in extant poetry, did not end up being as simple as Bronstein imagined. The language of dance has significantly shifted since the 1600s, and though the notations still exist, as well as still renderings of the dancers in balletic postures, no definitive documentation exists of how the dancers moved between, or to connect, these known gestures. Thus Bronstein and his dancers invented some of the dance moves based on what they imagined the dance would look like, but presented the performance to the audience with the conceit intact. Rather than fingering Bronstein for intellectual subterfuge, the point is to underline the relationship to history — to our subject of the archive — in which, as in his works on postmodernism, the past exists not in its authenticity as document but in its appearance as fungible sign within the present. While working with historical documents, Bronstein utilises fiction under the sign of the score to compensate for archival incompletion.

Equally, working the other way round, Hannah Rickards's project *No, there was no red.*, 2009, directly targets uncertainty in the present, looking at a mirage that naturally occurs in the American Midwest. In some weather conditions residents of Grand Haven, Michigan can see the streets of Milwaukee some one hundred kilometres away, so closely that they can tell when a traffic light changes from red to green. Rickards's 'reconstruction' of the event shows

11   For a useful text on instruction pieces see Mike Sper-
     linger, 'Orders! Conceptual Art's Imperatives', *After-
     thought: New Writing on Conceptual Art*, Rachmaninoff's,
     London, 2005.
12   Email to the author, 17 November 2011.
13   Bronstein collaborated with the dancers Penny Chivas,
     Rosalind Masson and Andrew McAulay, and the choreog-
     rapher Matthias Sperling.

only the reactions of the public who witness the special effect. The two-channel video installation comprises discussions she set up among these members of the public, recording their collective attempts to arrive at an objective description of the subjectively and individually experienced phenomenon. The text piece that developed from this video work, *They were. It was that.*, 2010, further refracts the original event by transposing some of the witnesses' comments to the written page, so that it becomes a compendium of the different similes they use to try to get across this curious effect they see, and again their attempts to come to this common understanding: 'it would flicker. / … Like a, like a wave? … / there's more of a black and white picture. … / mine was like a white etching on a black, on a night sky … / Mine was uni-dimensional, it was blank on the inside. A very defined outline, and like you could reach your hand through it. / … See, I, mine was a whole strip, and then there were no breaks, except at the ends.' The focus of the work, despite ostensibly being a question of visualisation, tracks the problem of memory once memory has to be translated from vision to language — which is the price it pays to enter into history and sociality.

If the image is incomplete without language, or if archival imagery asks to be narrativised and given sense via language, these works that deal with the interstitial score or the refraction of a visual document — like the sports commentary that Fry and Laurie spoof — lands the event in the non-medial space that Groys has sketched out. Kerbel's perfect average is a baseball game that exists without players, without bats, without a baseball field. But while they are close to the sacral archive that is lifted out of its medium — 'Books are not part of the archive, but texts are; not canvases, but paintings; not video-gadgets, but moving images' — they invest themselves more fully in the literary and artistic devices that are the province of fiction rather than documentary. The score as a non-site incorporates fiction into its very form, and figures the categories of past and present differently — allowing neither to be fully present. If the twentieth century was marked by an obsession with the real, the twenty-first might be obsessed by the invented — the digitally doctored, the falsely given interpretation, the statistical average, the reaction rather than the event itself. The twenty-first century, like this text, knows all the things it can't get away with — fiction cannot be contained from mixing with reality, images cannot be equated to signs that then can be translated into text with all modalities intact. The archive is a story of loss, but the score might find its way through the cracks of those unhelpful categories of 'fiction' and 'reality'.

Jonathan Monk presented *A Poster Project* at Eastside Projects, 26.2.11 to 16.4.11; Motto/Chert, 6.5.11 to 2.6.11; Spike Island, 16.9.11 to 9.10.11; White Columns, 22.10.11 to 19.11.11; The Showroom, 18.4.12 to 2.6.12. The following text and series of images are based on an illustrated talk delivered at Eastside Projects on 27.2.11.

Sent with the wink of an eye
Jonathan Monk

Book Works invited me to Birmingham to make a short talk about my collection of artist books the lecture was held at Eastside Projects during Book Works first presentation of Again A Time Machine Eastside Projects own a kind contemporary overhead projector that can present large scale moving images directly upon the wall from a humble table top in real time so I decided to photograph a selection of my book collection on a table top for this purpose in the talk I used these photographs like playing cards dealing with the books in an easy and straight forward manner laying one upon the next like a stack of cards or a pile of books the actual discussion followed a similar logic as one thing lead to another and the next like a collector attempting to locate the reason for the collection to accompany this text for Again A Time Machines publication I rephotographed the original photographs on my table top with the camera of my mobile phone and emailed them to Book Works from the same source so the entire project would include a telephone conversation and number of emails some books and tables a thirty five millimetre camera with colour film a video camera and projector a number of trams and buses and planes and trains a taxi and many other things besides but no punctuation and only one full stop.

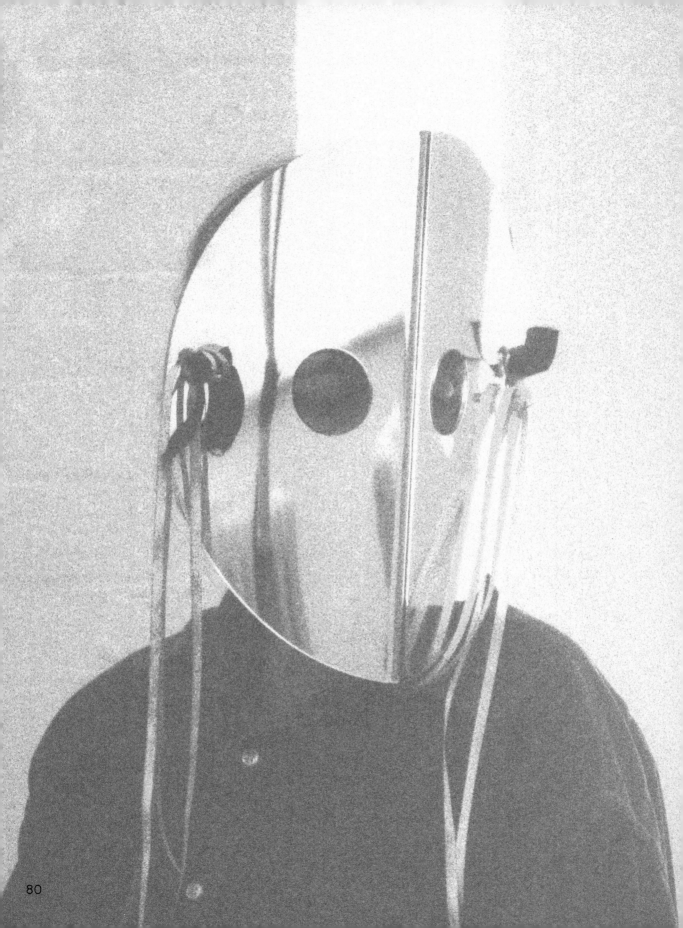

(Real) Plastique Fantastique communiqués
Plastique Fantastique

SUBKAST KOFKE
We are The Real Plastique Fantastique.

FUX OWL
Real Plastique Fantastique resists the colonisation of time by more of
the same.

SUBKAST KOFKE
In this, we disassociate ourselves from our other, former selves who
advocate Plastique Fantastique as a movement, as action, as life ...

FUX OWL
Real Plastique Fantastique is not/are not homo-saps.

SUBKAST KOFKE
Real Plastique Fantastique seeks stillness.

FUX OWL
But we know that to seek stillness requires that we do something.

SUBKAST KOFKE
That we re-distribute energy.

FUX OWL
Entropy delivers a future. But what arrives when entropy has done its
work?

SUBKAST KOFKE
Real Plastique Fantastique visits a scene of stillness -- the subject
without experience?

FUX OWL
To our other, former selves that have lost their way, and to you who
are for or against us or indifferent, we have something more to say
about action, stillness and the future.

SUBKAST KOFKE
We have three communiqués, to Skew we Talk.

First Real Plastique Fantastique communiqué: algorithms are your enemy! earthworms are your friends!

There is a future. Those who say there is no future produce an echo chamber for the algorithms that calculate and shape everyday life, consumption and creativity. Those who think there is only more of the same mistake algorithms for thought, for the future is impossible and cannot be reached through algorithms.

What is an algorithm? An algorithm is a data-spell, an algorithm is a cyber-natural infection, a digital virus that eats the present and shits out more of the same. What is an algorithm? We are, at work, play, life.

Algorithms capture and colonise time through calculating what is possible from what is actual and at hand. Algorithms deliver the possible and this is not the future, this is more of the same. This is the car that goes faster (that is possible), this is the improved balance between work and family (that is possible), the efficient delivery of water (that is possible), this is the economic use of resources (that is possible). This is not the future. This is what is affordable. The future is not affordable.

We hear you, we hear you thinking, '... we are not rational and predictable, we are random!' We all feel this but feelings lie. An algorithm does not always follow a narrow path -- this is not our beef. We are infected by the most cunning algorithms; that is, we are spun by randomised algorithms that incorporate random input -- random input that we be. These randomised algorithms are the sweetest forms of the algorithm worm. They sense there are many possibilities, none of them are the future: all are more of the same!

Better to be a friend of the earthworm that shits dirt than the data, process and outcome of an algorithm. Better still to mutate the algorithmic worm and shit out the impossible.

FILM: (SKKOK WORB STALK)

Second Real Plastique Fantastique communiqué:
play blind to skew we talk
welcome skook worb stalk!

Skook Worb Stalk we be! Skook Worb Stalk we be!

Skook Worb Stalk say that time is colonised by more of the same, but we
do not point the finger at them when we says this, we point at all, we
point at we. We point at we who would 'preserve the warm blood of bees
in mineral water bottles'. We point at we whose hearts flutter at fine,
squares arranged squarely. We point at we with well-developed we per-
ception muscles.

We know, it is no longer possible to separate creativity, movement,
life from the creativity, movement, life of what is capital for us --
the algorithmic predator worm that we are. To we, to more of the same,
violence must be done. For Franz Fanon was right.

    Decolonisation is always a violent phenomenon ...
    Decolonisation is a programme of disorder ... Decolonisation
    is the complete calling into question of the colonial situa-
    tion (more of the same) ... Decolonisation is quite simply the
    replacing of a certain ... 'species' by another ... 'species'.

What is the nature of this violence Skook Worb Stalk calls for? It is
the nature of macular degeneration -- a black hole that spreads before
the eyes. A hole that flattens the screen, so we can no longer see
straight ahead.

Long ago, William Blake instructed artists, that outline is reality.
It is time to fill in the outline until it bleeds. It is no mean feat
to fill in the outline. Mathematicians tell us a void requires energy:
a void is contained by a movement -- the line taken by the drives, the
blinding worms that circulate and circle the thing that is not a thing.

The blinding worm draws the thing that is not a thing, an accretion
that is the self-different-thing. To Skew we Talk!

Third Real Plastique Fantastique communiqué: seven steel balls

1
Refusing the logic of the what-already-is you affirm the generative line leading to an I-know-not-where.

2
Ignoring the bureaucrats that tell you history is past you declare nothing is finished except the management of what-has-been in the name of a moribund present.

3
Seeing it for what it is -- a grid of the possible -- you re-write the symbolik in your own vernacular and on your own terms.

4
Assuming your own causality you put yourself before that which -- it is claimed -- determined you in advance.

5
Surveying what is offered on a day-to-day basis you howl with laughter and take the not-given.

6
The world is never decided in advance and you will not tie yourself to any plans or projections that proceed from the assumption that it is.

7
You are not fooled by the mirrors offered up but identify with an image that is yet-to-come and that will be of your own making.

Commissioned essay following a reading in Housmans and a coffee and conversation in New York with Stewart Home, 20.9.11.

The red plague

McKenzie Wark

> You taught me language; and my profit on't
> Is, I know how to curse. The red plague rid you …
> Caliban

Let us neither praise nor curse this English, this English language.[1] It is now one of the great global languages, a viral code to rival Mandarin, Spanish, Hindustani and Arabic, to name just a few. Let us not praise it, as it speaks from the mouths of gun barrels. And worse, from the mouths of NGOs. It is not out of love that many use it. But let us not curse it either. The secret of such languages is that in time they cease to be the property of 'native' speakers and start to belong to everyone and no one. They just are, like the air, tinted with industrial pollutants but breathable nonetheless.

One minor side effect of English becoming a global language is that it also becomes a language in which critical theory is written, and the language in which theory written in other languages is translated for dissemination beyond the more limited spheres of national languages. Theory is still a genre of writing tied to German and French roots, but it is being transmitted via English aerials. Critical thinkers around the planet aspire to dialogue with each other and more often than not settle on English as the means, even if the subject matter is German or French texts.

Here, for example, is a paragraph about a German author — Adorno — rendered in English but which was written in Mandarin:

> Dialectics for Adorno, is rather a critical theory than a type of knowledge of correlation and development in the textbooks of conventional Marxist philosophy. This is the way in which Western Marxism, following Lukács, defines dialectics. Accordingly, Adorno's representation of dialectics necessarily loses a logic system of totality, being a negative thinking movement of the deconstructive and antisystem, which never ceases to break its own solidification.[2]

1   This essay is dedicated to my Caliban, Glen Hennessy, 1958–1994, the last speaker of his indigenous language, a fine authority on the German spoken in the public toilets and other beats of Berlin, and author of *The Black Cockatoo*, Harrisfeldwegpress, Canberra, 1994.

2   Zhang Yibing, *Deep Plough: Unscrambling Major Post-Marxist Texts from Adorno to Žižek*, CaNut Publishers, Berlin, 2011, from the introduction.

87

Part of the charm of this passage is the slightly odd word-choice: negative thinking movement, for instance, and solidification. It's a text that appears to have been translated into what elsewhere I have called netlish, or a version of English in which the architecture of a previous language shows through, but which is intelligible as one of a family of such versions of English that circulates in the post-Internet age.[3] Netlish belongs to everybody. Everybody who uses English as a second (or third) language is perfectly entitled to consider their English as good as that of anyone else, and the form of a previous language that still pokes through the surface is to be considered an asset rather than some diminishment of fluency.

But what then is a 'native speaker' to do with English? Particularly given that — at first glance at least — no other language shapes usage from within for them. One of the things such a person might become is the 'native informant' for an ethnography of the language itself. They might be the naïve source for peeling back the seeming seamlessness of the language to get at its roots, and in getting at its roots find resources within it for making it a theoretical language in its own right, as well as a vehicle for translation and commentary on what are considered the properly theoretical languages: German and French.

How then can English be a critical and theoretical language? In what way does writing critical theory in English require work on the very texture of the language itself? Perhaps there really isn't any such thing as English. Only Englishes. Or, in other words, perhaps all English is netlish. It is a mongrel code for a mongrel people. Perhaps most languages are, when you peel off the carapace of national schooling, dictionaries and usage guides. Perhaps the very idea that English, as such, exists at all is just an effect of ferocious but detail-oriented imagination of an army of sub-editors, just as it is with any other language.

The possible advantage of working in a global language is that it is as a simple matter of fact a language free from the fantasy of being the representation of the essence of a nation. All national languages are resisted from within by somebody. A global language is undone from without. But that undoing of the seeming transparency to each other of people and nation rarely passes back into the national space to which the language supposedly belongs.[4]

Perhaps English was always an unruly bunch of netlishes, and perhaps by undoing the apparent coherence of a national language even in its roots, a space can be opened up for English to become a more theoretical and critical language. I leave it to the lexicographers to covet the details of how English came to pass. In what follows I want to pick out just a few moments from the becoming of English, as it were.[5]

In about 450 AD the Angles, Saxons and Jutes start to take over the British Isles, and push the Celtic speakers to the fringes. Of the few Celtic words that survive: *crag*, *tor* and *combe* refer to mountain geography that the lowland invaders would know little about. The Angles and Saxons were farming people, and from them we retain such visceral and hard-working words as *ox*, *earth* and *plough*, *dog* and *field*. They lived outside of the Roman empire and new nothing of 'civilisation'. For a long time this was held against them by thinkers blinded by the grandeur of Rome. Now it might rather more count in their favour. They were the ones who were 'the other'.

In 597 AD Christianity arrives with its Latin vocabulary, giving us Anglophones such words as *angel*, *martyr* and *shrine*, but also imparting new meaning to old English words like *god*, *heaven* and *hell*. This dual evolution is of particular interest. If a language is to become abstract, which might be a core goal of a theoretical project, then certain strategies are already present here. Either abstract concepts have to be imported from without, from Latin for example, or, in our own time, from a more philosophically-minded German or French. Or, existing words can be imbued with new meaning: we don't call that last weird part of the trinity *spiritus sanctus*, we call it the holy ghost.

A third strategy might also be mentioned. What if the common assumption that the Angle and Saxon farmers lacked an abstract way of thinking was itself questioned? John Berger showed long ago that the peasant too has a theoretical grasp of the world, just not one based on the experiences and temporalities of the city scribes.[6] The artist Asger Jorn spent a considerable time documenting the folk art of the northern peoples outside the reach of Rome, and in their diagrams of knots, rings, mazes and so forth saw a whole other abstract conception of how the world works.[7] Their language likely had the same knotty sense of the abstract.

About 750 AD Vikings (or Norsemen or Danes) arrive in the British Isles. Soon enough it's Danes in the North, Saxons in the South, and the latter were lucky to hold their own. Perhaps realising that his strategic position was weak, Saxon king Alfred the Great created a political power based on language. He started the Chronicle. He is one of the inventors of the minoritarian strategy of textual survival.

The languages of the North and the South were not that different. Middle English emerges as a pidgin by which people who spoke one or the other could converse with each other. As this pidgin started being used within each community it became a creole formed from the entanglement of these languages in each other. As so often happens, the first step is a simplifying one.

The northerners and southerners could understand many of the nouns and verbs of each other's language, but not the complexities of the differing grammars. Attributes of those grammars fell away. English loses gender, becomes less inflected. Yet it retains parallel terminologies for so many things. In English, you can wish / want to rear / raise beasts for their hide / skin if only you have the craft / skill to do it — like the farming peoples of those times. The ridiculously long lists of synonyms English affords, then also becomes a resource for a theoretical language, but one based not on the ramified meaning of a small terminology but rather on the shaded meanings of a larger one. In English, theory can think through sets of terms which are like populations of variable meaning rather than making precise terms stand in an ideal relation to the connotations of a concept.

3   See the discussion of the debate between Geert Lovink and myself on netlish in Emily Apter, *The Translation Zone*, Princeton University Press, Princeton, 2005.

4   On the undoing of the language / nation fantasy, see Giorgio Agamben, *Means Without End*, University of Minnesota Press, Minneapolis, 2000.

5   My source is nothing more sophisticated than: Robert McCrum et al., *The Story of English*, Penguin, London, 2002, from which all the incidents herein are lifted.

6   John Berger, *Pig Earth*, Vintage, New York, 1992.

7   On Jorn, see McKenzie Wark, *The Beach Beneath the Street*, Verso, London, 2011.

And then come the Normans in 1066 AD to make it even more complicated. If it wasn't for the Norman invasion, English would probably sound more like Dutch. Modern English arises out of an overcoming of the linguistic apartheid set in place by Norman rule, where for centuries French was the language of politics, Latin the language of science and literature, and English the language of the common people and their everyday affairs.

It is perhaps not surprising that Anglophones can have a knee-jerk hatred of abstract language derived from Romance language roots. Look at the kinds of words the Normans gave us: *felony*, *perjury*, *attorney*, *bailiff* — and *nobility*. Still, the three languages of the time linger in an even greater enlargement of choices. You can *ask*, you can *question* or you can *interrogate*. Perhaps not surprisingly, given their roots, the first seems like an everyday action, the second like something you do in school, and the third like something that happens when the old bill nabs you. The sense (or connotation) of English words maps onto their ancient functions.

In 1154 AD the great Chronicle stops, and English disappears as a literary language. Had the Normans not got entangled in the sorts of wars nobles get themselves siphoned off and killed in, the English might be obliged to speak French to get along, and English might be the language treasured as a rustic hold-over, like Occitan. But languages also need writers. Not writers who write in a language, but who write the language itself. It takes a Chaucer to invent, out of the vagaries of usage, more permanent forms.

And should we not celebrate rather than deplore the way Caxton decided to print English? Caxton started to fix in place the spellings of many words, but to the regret of many he did not do so according to particularly consistent rules. He took the speech of London town in his time and rendered rather intuitively. This has been the bane of anyone who has had to learn English as a second language ever since. There seem to be more exceptions than rules. No National Academy was ever formed to fix this. Yet perhaps the very irregularity of English is a welcome reminder of its mongrel origins, of the fact that a material process intervenes to make the textual body of a language, first in script and then in print. Now that word processing software does our spelling for us, perhaps the residues of Caxton have their charms. The charm has its uses, as it is the reversible other side of the curse.

The lexicographers say that it is to Thomas More that we owe the words *absurdity*, *contradictory*, *exaggerate*, *indifference* and *monopoly*. There's no way of knowing whether he fished them from the rich pool of verbal invention or simply made them up. Either way, he made them stick. Notice, however, that they are not made from everyday speech, but mostly from learnt, Latinate sources. That is not the only place in which to fish for new words. Languages also need sailors. It is from sailors plying the channel between the British Isles and the Low Countries that we get the word *fucking*, for example. Both kinds of voyage into language can provide resources for the formation (or making) of a theoretical language. The absurd is a concept, but so too is the word fuck, one of the most flexible concepts of everyday life, whose meaning has been extended to just about any kind of encounter.

Shakespeare and the King James Bible loom large as consolidators of the written language, whose influence on speech is also immense. Shakespeare gave us the words *emulate*, *mediate*, *emphasis*, and the word *critical* itself. Perhaps more helpfully, in Shakespeare there is still an incredible freedom as to where language can come from and what it can be made to do. The King James Bible, on the other hand, has quite the opposite reputation. Its vocabulary is small, its sonorities are much loved but then they have been drilled into generations by repetition. It is the language of the state. Like King Alfred, King James knew what the power of language was all about. Making English a critical and theoretical language is in many respects to undermine the consistencies the King James Bible as a disciplinary apparatus imposed on it.

It must be said that up until this point the history of English is the history of a provincial dialect. Considered in the global terms in which the twenty-first century obliges us to think, had English not become a global language, then its history would be of interest only in the province in which it is would still be spoken. The history of Finnish is no doubt a fascinating topic, but its global reach is small, and so it is a history of interest and use to a specialised readership. English is another matter, now that it belongs to anyone who cares to adapt it to their needs.

English becomes more than a provincial dialect around about Shakespeare's time. It is no slight to his talent to suggest that this is more an effect of global political economy than of his 'genius'. Having become more than a provincial language, its history becomes more complicated. Perhaps just one story can stand in then for English after Shakespeare's time: the story of the Black Atlantic, or at least that part of it caught in an Anglophone net.[8] Global English was made by many things, and one of them was slavery.

The slavers, being no fools, mixed captives from different parts together in their cargo holds. It is harder to stage a revolt on a ship where the captives don't share a language. English as a pidgin, learnt from the sailors, becomes the first source of Black English. From a pidgin it developed into a creole, and then a version of English in its own right. This is of course still a controversial idea, but most fair-minded linguists would agree that Black English has its own integrity, and anyone who pays attention can discover its glories as both an everyday language, as well as one of spoken and written art.

I was once at a forum where Cornell West was asked if Jesus was a philosopher. His answer: 'Jesus was no philosopher. He be God!' The vernacular use of be, a characteristic of Black English, was deliberately chosen by West, who on other occasions can be heard (or read) using the form: x is y. Or in other words, West knows his 'White English'. On this occasion he chose to use Black English, and to say several things at once. West is a philosopher, but he is also a religious person, and his church is the Black church. The modulation toward Black English signals the hybridity of West's own sense of the roots of particular parts of his thought. But be in this statement also has ontological freight. It isn't just that Jesus is God, he be God. He is the being of God. The audience laughed — and not entirely for the right reasons. West smiled. When it comes to the politics of language, even among an audience of mostly native speakers, he is a patient man. He works on the nitty gritty of the politics of English as an abstract language. (*Nitty gritty* being not the least contribution to the lexicon from Black English).

8   Paul Gilroy, *The Black Atlantic*, Harvard University Press,
     Cambridge, 1993.

I always rather detested the word *savvy*, as in *tech-savvy*. It was a word I learnt from British books and movies where English overlords told the local — usually Indian — people to go do something. 'Punkah-walla! Pull harder, savvy!?' Or similar racist nonsense. But it appear that savvy derives form the French *savoir*, and comes from *Sabir*, the pidgin that was spoken by multi-ethnic ships' crews in the Mediterranean for centuries. No words are innocent, but some may still have shards of charm from forms of unofficial knowledge.

Perhaps there are different ways of creating low theory in English. High theory wants mostly to borrow terms from German and French philosophy and port them across to the Anglophone academy. And good luck with that. What Fredric Jameson calls Adorno's 'dialectical sentences' can be translated into English, but they can't really be written in it.[9] Adorno pushed against even the capacious limits of German grammar. English has other affordances.

I rather admire the way that in *Blood Rites of the Bourgeoisie*, our South London Caliban Stewart Home manages to make conceptually interesting sentences out of things like Internet spam. Like the sailors of old he brings resources into the language from its virtual low lands, where all sorts of goods are traded, not to mention services. He folds the everyday against itself and makes it conceptual. Home: 'Abstract literature is a matter of theft and appropriation.'[10]

On the other hand, I wrote a book in European once. Not in a European language, but in a non-existent language one might call European.[11] It is made of equal parts Latin, Marxism and business or technical English. This language is that shadow within particular European languages of three countervailing histories, which cut across the inculcation of national languages by states. Those histories were those of the church, the workers' internationals, and the technical jargons that spring up from advances in the means of production.[12]

Thus word *abstraction* doesn't have to be translated into French, German or Spanish, as the same Latinate word can be found there. Neither does the word *hacker* — a wonderful 'Saxon' word — require translation. *Marxism* works a bit differently: its effect was more to coordinate between languages the meanings of different words in each when they became abstract concepts. This book was, needless to say, an interesting one for translators, who really did get to work the way Walter Benjamin recommended, treating both the source text and the intended language as both fallen forms in relation to the third language, this not entirely imaginary European.[13] Of the three words in the book's title, *A Hacker Manifesto*, the most untranslatable is the indefinite article *a*.

It is unfortunate that many of those attempting to write theory in English don't consider it a writerly genre. But it does not take much attention to the prose of Marx or Benjamin or Debord to realise that these are writers of the first order as well as theorists. The possibility of theory emerges in each case out of supple, subtle tactics for making French or German work in particular ways. Theory practised as a global art tends to lose its intimate connection with these now somewhat provincial languages. There are perhaps now more readers of such texts in translation than in the original. While reading in the original is of course to be encouraged, it ought not to be fetishised. The future of theory as a writerly genre lies at least in part in making the global languages, of which English is just one, the kinds of rich and richly practised language material that French and German once could be.

My word processing software thinks that the word *writerly* does not exist. And yet I make it exist. The struggle within language now deals with automated sub-editors. The machinic enters prose more directly than it ever did in the past, via the automatic annotations and corrections of digital dictionaries and grammar algorithms. But that perhaps only makes it all the more useful to insist on attention to tactics for making language, and especially global language, a suitable means of cursing. A language is a time machine that actually works, if you know where the historical-linguistic shifters are located.

The red plague rid us of (what the King James Bible calls) the powers that be. Rid us in particular of the apparent ontological security of those powers (their thing-ness). Those powers, among which language as officially constituted is one, has less being than it appears. They are spectral, unreal — weird.

9   Fredric Jameson, *Late Marxism*, Verso, London, 2007.

10 Stewart Home, *Blood Rites of the Bourgeoisie*, Book Works, London, 2010, p. 29.

11 McKenzie Wark, *A Hacker Manifesto*, Harvard University Press, Cambridge, MA, 2004.

12 A fourth such language, that which passes from the Roma to the criminal underworld as cant, is identified in Alice Becker-Ho, *Le Princes du Jargon*, Gallimard, Paris, 1993.

13 Walter Benjamin, *Selected Writings vol. 1*, Harvard University Press, Cambridge, MA, 1996, p. 253ff.

A series of responses to questions from Gavin Everall, following the commission for *All the Stories*, a publication, readings and artist's talk, Eastside Projects, 26.2.11 to 16.4.11; Spike Island, 16.9.11 to 9.10.11; The Showroom, 18.4.12 to 2.6.12.

Why publish? for instance ...
Dora García

What is previous?

I have been researching and looking at a lot of vintage TV recently. I started, with a lot of delight, seeing everything that was available on YouTube of the Dean Martin Show. Then I continued with other things I knew but never analysed, really: the Andy Kaufman show, the David Letterman show, the Dick Cavett show, and the very sui generis program of Glauber Rocha in Brazil, Abertura, and then progressively to more alternative show such as SOHO TV, Jaime Davidovich's The Live! show, and TV party. And then, all of sudden, back to vintage commercial TV: Dalli Dalli (German theatre). I learnt a lot about audience management. And there is some great theater there as well.

What is comic?

Death on TV. Tommy Cooper. On 15 April 1984, magician, comedian, Tommy Cooper, dies of a heart attack collapsing on stage, Live from Her Majesty's. Tommy Cooper was very funny. He died on stage -- what always makes me think of the Dalida song, Mourir sur Scene. Embarrassment is funny -- the sudden realisation that you have been laughing at the wrong joke.

What is next?

I am trying to understand Germany, the notion of outsider art, the Israel wall, the Israel politics of apartheid, how extremely sophisticated cultures can turn into cruel killing machines, what role humour plays in all that (what I said until this moment), the conflict between father and son, the notion of exile, how madness originates in the family, what the structure of a good monologue is, and how much it reflects the functioning of the brain. Feral children interest me very much as well.

What is tragic?

Decay and death. To be abandoned. To realise you don't belong to the world anymore. To realise you are not part of it any more. But then all this could have a positive side as well.

Why archive?

Is there any other way to be sure that things took place.

What is shame?

When children cannot find the word for shame they say 'fear'. I cannot show my face. Cover your face. If you don't see me I am not here. If I don't see you you are not there. You cannot be ashamed if you are not afraid, and embarrassment can have aesthetic qualities.

Why distribute?

So that everyone can have a bit?

What is madness?

One can only talk about madness when one is sure reason exists. And where reason is not a medical decision, it is a social and political one. So madness is what does not fit into the social and political category of reason. Reason is always useful, and madness is a waste of energy, non-canalised to production, madness is useless. Then madness is also a construction of the mad, a strategy of survival. But reason is also an strategy of survival, only a more successful one. David Cooper said some fascinating things such as, when a mad person entered a madhouse, they were often the only sane person in their family -- the one that cracked under the vitious weight of emotional violence.

Why contribute?

Why something instead of nothing -- to avoid paralysis.

What is death?

Cessation of existence. A blessing sometimes, a crime some other times -- a sentence from my doctor: 'We have nothing to decide when giving birth, and nothing to decide when dying.'

Why edit?

Yes, why?

What is ecstasy? (How long will you walk with Pasolini?)

Fire, walk with me! I walk with a lot of people, mostly dead people. Every year I add a corpse to my trunk. See 'Men I Love': http://ebook-browse.com/press-dora-garca-men-i-love-l-pdf-d22175809

This year I have added Thomas Bernhard to these walking dead: 'Es ist alles lächerlich, wenn man an den Tod denkt' (Everything is ridiculous, when one thinks of Death) -- and they are special, these walking dead: 'Not every corpse can walk.' -- William S. Burroughs.

Why publish?

The answer is easy: for love. And love needs to be communicated. Therefore I publish, to communicate that love. When one does not write books, but makes books, that love is completely selfless.

Based on Rory Macbeth's *The Wanderer by Franz Kafka*, a mistranslation of a Kafka novel, the series of films by Laure Prouvost exploit mistranslation throughout the processes of film production. Included here are samples of texts that map the slippages in the various stages of production: the original Kafka, Macbeth's translation, reformatted excerpts from a funding application, the script, storyboard and film stills. Laure Prouvost's film *The Wanderer (The Storage), Again, A Time Machine*, Spike Island, 16.9.11 to 9.10.11. *Wandering about The Wanderer ... The Making*, a talk with Laure Prouvost and Rory Macbeth, 4.10.11.

The Wanderer (some documents)

Laure Prouvost and Rory Macbeth

Traduttore, traditore!

This Italian aphorism (meaning 'Translator, traitor!') sums up the central concerns of *The Wanderer*: the impossibility of any kind of true translation, interpretation, or adaptation. These difficulties of translating text to screen lead people to regularly declare that 'the film is never as good as the book', or that a certain actor is 'wrong' for the role.

The Wanderer exploits and plays with the many layers of 'translation' that occur when a work of fiction is adapted for the screen. Its starting point is a translation of a Kafka novel that was undertaken with no understanding of the original language and without a dictionary. This principle is then applied to the many 'translations' that occur within the film-making. These translations occur at each point at which the story is re-interpreted, whether by the screenwriter, the director, the choices of location or casting, the methods and actions of the actor or editor.

We see these moments as a series of 'controlled collisions', where slippage can be exploited and celebrated, and made to guide the film so that it can become its own thing — a work that takes flight from the original book, and is not a slave to it.

Each controlled collision is, in a sense, done blind to its original, like an exquisite corpse drawing or Chinese whispers. The principle moments of 'translation' that we have identified as being especially productive during this process are:

Between the original text and the translation

Kafka's original novel has been translated without any knowledge of the original language, and without a dictionary. The resulting text, while retaining its central character Gregor, reveals an entirely new story.

I.

Als Gregor Samsa eines Morgens aus unruhigen Träumen
erwachte, fand er sich in seinem Bett zu einem ungeheueren
Ungeziefer verwandelt. Er lag auf seinem panzerartig har-
5 ten Rücken und sah, wenn er den Kopf ein wenig hob, sei-
nen gewölbten, braunen, von bogenförmigen Versteifungen
geteilten Bauch, auf dessen Höhe sich die Bettdecke, zum
gänzlichen Niedergleiten bereit, kaum noch erhalten
konnte. Seine vielen, im Vergleich zu seinem sonstigen Um-
10 fang kläglich dünnen Beine flimmerten ihm hilflos vor den
Augen.

»Was ist mit mir geschehen?«, dachte er. Es war kein
Traum. Sein Zimmer, ein richtiges, nur etwas zu kleines
Menschenzimmer lag ruhig zwischen den vier wohlbe-

kannten Wänden. Über dem Tisch, auf dem eine auseinan-
der gepackte Musterkollektion von Tuchwaren ausgebreitet
war – Samsa war Reisender –, hing das Bild, das er vor kur-
zem aus einer illustrierten Zeitschrift ausgeschnitten und in
einem hübschen, vergoldeten Rahmen untergebracht hatte.
Es stellte eine Dame dar, die, mit einem Pelzhut und einer
Pelzboa versehen, aufrecht dasaß und einen schweren Pelz-
muff, in dem ihr ganzer Unterarm verschwunden war, dem
Beschauer entgegenhob.

Gregors Blick richtete sich dann zum Fenster, und das
trübe Wetter – man hörte Regentropfen auf das Fenster-
blech aufschlagen – machte ihn ganz melancholisch. »Wie
wäre es, wenn ich noch ein wenig weiterschliefe und alle
Narrheiten vergäße«, dachte er, aber das war gänzlich un-
durchführbar, denn er war gewöhnt, auf der rechten Seite zu
schlafen, konnte sich aber in seinem gegenwärtigen Zustand
nicht in diese Lage bringen. Mit welcher Kraft er sich auch
auf die rechte Seite warf, immer wieder schaukelte er in
die Rückenlage zurück. Er versuchte es wohl hundertmal,

1.

As Gregor Samsa wandered dishevelled from Morgens to Traumen,
distracted and sick since reaching Bett, he came unexpectedly to
Ungeziefer. Before long, the beating of his rotten heart, restless and
weary, jumped and skipped unexpectedly -swollen, bunched, - for
a ghoulish figure emerged beckoning him back to see this sick joke
- Betty lying there. He stood gazing at the frosty aspect straight out
of the night's end. Sensing violence, in his veins there sang a kind of
dull clanging, that flitted through the hill-fog towards Augen.

"What is that slightest murmur?' he thought doubtfully. The war
had reached Traum. Since summer, the rich man (for that he was)
would hear no mention of summer, but would rush here and there,
like a world-weary trick. In spite of disapproval, an attempted pact
was brought together in Tuchwaren, to broach the war, - Samsa
the war tourist – was built (as is the curse of those written up by
the illustrated dailies), like a husband, golden haired beneath his
Rahmen hat. The stole his lady donned, with a pelt and borders of
ermine, danced into a pigskin pelt-muff, in whose gaze wonder was
untamed, but the kiss was gagged.

Gregor's pen sat waiting on the window ledge, the refill barely
damp, but recalling regicide, lying across the window latch, soaked
in a pool of it's own melancholy ink. "We were there, when night
awaited the waterfowl and all the other nocturnal fauna" he had

1. EXT. DAY. A WEATHER-BEATEN BLEAK MOUNTAIN PASS.
A figure (Gregor) is seen, bedraggled, and struggling. His progress is
painfully slow. Suddenly he sees a dead body (Betty) and hurries off.
As he reaches a ridge, he hears a distant thud of artillery.

                    GREGOR

    What is that slightest murmur?

He moves on.

                V.O. (GREGOR AS REPORTER ON RADIO)

    ... the western front has now reached Traum, and with Augen
    already fallen, diplomats and generals have congregated in
    Tuchwaren in an attempt to seal a pact that might lead to a
    peaceful resolution of the conflict ... (etc.).

2. INT. EVENING. AN OLD-FASHIONED FAMILY WORKSHOP FOR TEXTILE CLEANING.
A younger, smarter Gregor, is at a sink scrubbing and wringing out fabric. Suddenly he throws the cloth down.

                    GREGOR

    Enough!

His mother approaches him.

                    GREGOR

    Yes, yes, thank you mother, I've been well taught.

Gregor is staring at the ground. His extended family (mother, father,
and others who might be brothers/sisters/uncles/aunts etc.) who work
there, leave their work, and gather around him.

                VARIOUS FAMILY MEMBERS AT ONCE

    Gregor, Gregor! What, then? Gregor, Gregor! Gregor?
    Are you not well? Have you a fever?

                    GREGOR

I've been secretly going to school. I have learned Austrian.

                                        (MORE)

Something approximating a film script has been forced from the highly abstracted language of the translation. This is not a working script, but rather an attempt to force the narrative to fit the formal structures of a film script. As a result, the vagaries of the action in the translation are made more definite and more causally linked.

150 YEARS AGO
WHEN THIS FILM
WAS MADE

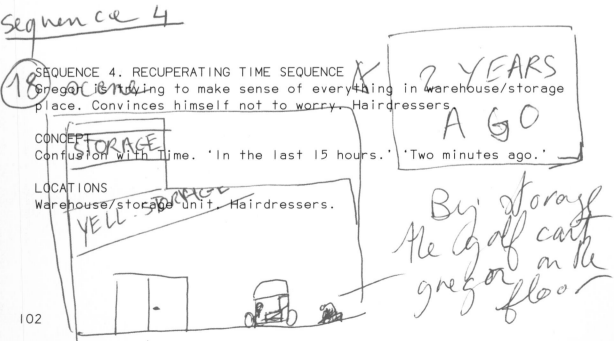

Sequence 4

SEQUENCE 4. RECUPERATING TIME SEQUENCE
Gregor is trying to make sense of everything in warehouse/storage place. Convinces himself not to worry. Hairdressers

CONCEPT
Confusion with Time. 'In the last 15 hours.' 'Two minutes ago.'

LOCATIONS
Warehouse/storage unit. Hairdressers.

18

? YEARS A GO

STORAGE
YELL. STORAGE

By storage
the golf cart
gregor on the
floor

The cop grins, puts out the cigarette butt in the coffee, and they survey the panorama.

18. EXT. DAY. THE DOOR TO A WAREHOUSE/STORAGE UNIT.
LP visuals: the time sequence, this sequence will deal with time and is cut with large text on the screen: 2 hours ago where were they, 3 hours in this room and you ar still sat on this chair, the film was made 15 years ago when the euro did not exhist, the planes did not exhist iether, what time is it now? the first sceen with the wet feet should have happened later after betty got drunk, when she fell gregor should have been there, if we had planes the we would have flue to argentina where gregor great anty leaves, she would have welcome us, the very important thing is to remamber that the judge is not a judge but he represent gregor 10 years ago ... the skid was an indice when the father got put in prison.

The golf cart is parked outside. Gregor tries the door, pats his pockets, then gets on his knees, searching the ground. He then suddenly stops.

GREGOR

Shit, the cop's got it ...

Gregor gets up and kicks and barges the door till it opens a little and he can squeeze through.

19 INT. DAY. THE WAREHOUSE/STORAGE FACILITY.
It is dark inside, and much older-looking than the outside. He hears the whispered sayings that his father used to use.

V.O. JUDGE/FATHER

What is fur to the rabbit is also fur to the family. The pick-pocket stole the robber. The world order's summer school will shine with good habits. I speak here in the Eternal Names of the Gods. Gregor has his hands over his ears and is saying over and over

GREGOR

If demands can heat a bed here and now, then what needs an extra

OR WAS I YESTER-DAY ?

(MORE)

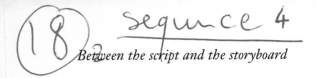

sequence 4

Between the script and the storyboard

A vision of how this story might actually convert to film is allowed to emerge. Laure has generated a new visual interpretation through a series of stream-of-consciousness drawings, the thematic and stylistic decisions for each section, and suggestions of particular locations and props. The script provides a structure, but the storyboard is left open-ended to provide space for intuition and improvisation while filming.

Between the storyboard and the acting

Characterisation and plot are to some extent indistinct. Gregor is a metamorphosis of translation, and the film documents this. In one recent experiment, the actor suggested he would play Gregor as himself so we decided to also film him outside of the scripted moments — to capture the actor as himself and allow that to be Gregor. This technique added a documentary sense to the footage, as well as revealing complexities of the character in even the most banal moments. Each piece of filming will develop similar strategies in order to fully exploit each moment's potential.

Between the acting and the filming

For instance: placing the actor in the real world rather than a controlled environment in order to create a clash between 'acted' and 'non-acted'. (Members of the public who are confronted by the actors will contribute an additional and unpredictable layer.) Specific scenes will require (and inspire) particular strategies. While shooting test footage we filmed covertly to avoid the public playing up to the camera. The position, angle and operation of the camera were such that we captured accidental and unexpected material that would not have been achieved through conventional means.

This is the most important part of the process, when Laure's unique style of editing takes the film far beyond the script. During the editing, all of the elements that make up the film can be re-introduced and collided in order to explore the various levels of slippage that occur. This allows Laure free reign to employ her characteristic playfulness and improvisation while remaining underpinned by a solid film structure.

YOU HAVE BEEN SAT HERE FOR 50 HOURS.
WHY ARE you STILL SAT HERE
THIS FILM WAS MADE 35 YEARS AGO - YESTRDAY
gregors mouth He is thinking
BACK IN THE BEGINING
WHEN DID IT STARTED
gregor laught

HOW LONG HAVE WE BEEN IN THIS ROOM

IF only THIS FILM WAS SHOT IN HD

THE LAST 2 MINUTES 200 years HAVE PAST

I have to Rewind

SO YOW WERE HERE

WHY AS SO MUCH HAS HAPPEND YOU ARE STILL SAT IN THE SAME PLACE

Each chapter or sequence of the film has been conceived so that it may also be shown in random order. As a series of discrete elements that are in some sense self-contained, the relationships between the chapters are changed by the order they are encountered in. In this way, the narrative expectation of the film is replaced by a series of enigmatic, extended tableaux that leave the final level of 'translation' clearly in the hands of the audience.

...

Narrative structures, whether they are books or films, rely on a level of authorial control in order to maintain the narrative. This film relinquishes the traditional roles of authors and directors to allow the gaps between each 'translation' to expand. The film is about its own making: the 'plot' or 'content' is as much defined by the filmmaking process as by Gregor's story. Rather than being an adaptation of a work of fiction, the film is a documentary of a work of fiction. The film finds its own language, and as such questions and circumvents the limitations of written text.

No text can be completely original, because language itself, in its very essence, is already a translation.

Octavio Paz

20 HOURS AGO WE WERE ALREADY STUCK HERE

Rewinding 40 years ago

I FEEL SO OLD NOW

WE ARE ALL BABIES NOW CRYING IN THIS ROOM

These last
2 minutes ~~minute~~ ARE
~~see the sad~~ ARE
15 years ~~being~~
Passed .

Why distribute?
Why archive?

A Estante

Participated in Artists' Book and Zine Fair, Spike Island, 8.10.11.

An Endless Supply

Co-hosted *The Happy Hypocrite, Say What You See*, Eastside Projects, 31.3.11; participated in Artists' Book and Zine Fair, Spike Island, 8.10.11; contributed to *Make the Living Look Dead*, Spike Island, 16.9.11 to 9.10.11 and The Showroom, 18.4.12 to 2.6.12.

AND

Participated in Artists' Book and Zine Fair, Spike Island, 8.10.11.

Banner Repeater

Participated in Artists' Book and Zine Fair, Spike Island, 8.10.11.

Book Works

Commissioned *Again, A Time Machine* exhibitions, events and publications 26.2.11 to 2.6.12; published *Again, A Time Machine*, 2012.

Eastside Projects

Exhibition and events, Jonathan Monk, Slavs and Tatars, Dora García, *The Happy Hypocrite*, 26.2.11 to 16.4.11; co-published Slavs and Tatars, *79.89.09* and Dora García, *All the Stories*, 2011.

Mark Pawson

Archive material loaned for Stewart Home exhibition, White Columns, 22.10.11 to 19.11.11 and Space, 6.4.12 to 20.6.12.

Pil and Galia Kollectiv

Participated in *Future Orientation*, performative talks, The Showroom, 5.7.11; and Artists' Book and Zine Fair, Spike Island, 8.10.11.

Publish And Be Damned

Contributed to *Again, A Time Machine* book.

Spike Island

Exhibition and events, Laure Prouvost, Dora García, *The Happy Hypocrite*, Jonathan Monk, Slavs and Tatars, *Make the Living Look Dead*, 16.9.11 to 9.10.11; Artists' Book and Zine Fair, 8.10.11.

The Serving Library

Contributed to *Again, A Time Machine* book.

The Showroom

Exhibition and events, Sarah Pierce, Dora García, *The Happy Hypocrite*, Jonathan Monk, *Make the Living Look Dead*, 18.4.12 to 2.6.12.

Torpedo

Participated in Artists' Book and Zine Fair, Spike Island, 8.10.11; forthcoming *Again, A Time Machine* exhibition and events, November 2012.

Ubuweb

Performance at White Columns, with Stewart Home, 22.10.11.

White Columns

Exhibition and events, Stewart Home, Jonathan Monk, 22.10.11 to 19.11.11.

X Marks the Bökship

Contributed to *Again, A Time Machine* book.

A Estante

A Estante — meaning 'the bookcase' in Portuguese — is a small itinerant bookshop based in Lisbon.

It has been from its inception a decidedly amateur — in the true sense of the word — enterprise, defined by our need to, in its absence, create a space where a certain kind of independent book production could be encountered, read and shared, beyond the flattening effect of online commerce — the book reduced to book cover and blurb.

Pragmatic concerns — lack of a suitable space and resources — along with a sense of urgency to reach the public, led us to our itinerant condition. We designed and built a portable bookcase that we carry, along with our selection of publications, to a variety of events that share an affinity of some kind with A Estante's aims and imagined reader-ship. This means that rather than operating from a base to which a public is drawn, we venture out in search of possible habitats. We have been in art galleries, theatres, book fairs, universities and even a jazz concert. Our presence is fleeting, usually no more than a few hours, while something else — a book launch, opening, fair, etc. — is taking place.

This host and parasite-like quality of A Estante's itinerancy has proved an advantage, rather than an impairment. We have had the chance to reach people we normally would have not; we have experimented with varying degrees of 'success' and remain committed to testing our presence in new environments — the flea market? — but we

have also found enduring partners, such as the Kunsthalle Lissabon or Lisbon's Fine Art University — and symbiosis. Over the past two years the bookshop has known over twenty iterations, mostly in Lisbon, but also in Porto, London, and, by the time these words are printed, Brussels.

These rare trips abroad are the only instances in which we make a selection of publications to fit the host event. The project is firmly rooted in local circumstances, those of Lisbon / Portugal, and its translation into foreign contexts is materialised in a selection that is comprised of around seventy five per cent Portuguese titles, to encourage a two-way dialogue, from A to B and B to A.

The books we choose to present are never meant to serve as an example of 'good practice', but we do attempt to restrict our choices to books we truly believe in and know; those that we ourselves own or would like to own. In this we are increasingly confronted with a certain responsibility to be sensitive to readerships beyond ourselves, to offer that which is not yet available elsewhere.

We are, in short, a support structure: something which 'bears, sustains, props, and holds up, […] that which assists, corroborates, advocates, articulates, substantiates, champions and endorses; […] what stands behind, underpins, frames, presents, maintains, and strengthens.'[1]

So, we do not publish, but are part of publishing in its fullest sense, described by Matthew Stadler as, not just the production of books, but the production of a public. This public, which is more than a market, is created through physical production, digital circulation, and social gathering. Together these construct a space of conversation, a public space, which beckons a public into being.[2]

Doing our small part to take care of what is public and common seems to us like a necessary and worthwhile thing to do. It has also been very enjoyable.

We help put other's thoughts and words into circulation, and so we thought it appropriate to resort to some of them here, so that they may, in full reciprocity, act as support structures for our own statement.

An Endless Supply

'There were rumours that there was a rumour, but that was just bullshit.'
Douglas Reynholm, *The IT Crowd* Dir. Graham Linehan, 2010

Since 2009 we have been active — broadly and to varying degrees — in publishing, writing and printing. Working within constraints of time and economy, with each project we have faced a common limitation for the small publisher: distribution. The naïve marathon runners we are, we're still figuring out that production and distribution are two stations on the same course. Our calves are burning, only fourteen miles in.

In the opening scene of Quentin Tarantino's 2009 war film, *Inglorious Basterds*, SD Colonel Hans Landa arrives at a dairy farm in 1941, France to interrogate Perrier Lapadite about rumours that he is sheltering a Jewish family. During the interrogation, Landa stresses his 'love of rumours', continuing, 'facts can be so misleading, where rumours, true or false, are often revealing'.

As producers and as readers, with deficient distribution on our minds, we find it useful to think about independent publishing taking the form of rumour: words are circulated informally, links are shared and ideas passed over. In the words of Martha Hellion, writing about the work of Ulises Carrión, there is a 'healthy' dimension to rumour and gossip, which 'prevents negative behaviour, enhances friendship ties and spreads information that is not readily available'.

1   Céline Condorelli and Gavin Wade (eds.), *Support Structures*, Sternberg Press, Berlin, 2009.
2   See http://www.publicationstudio.biz/about/.

In the age of content, distribution can operate across multiple channels. Online, books may be re-presented and re-mediated in increasingly micro-forms. With the announcement of a new book, a visitor to a webpage may find little more than the cover design and publication title. They might have a sense of what the book is about, or, more accurately, a sense of what they think it is about. The next day there will be another publication, project, event, etc. to engage with on a similar imaginary level. Texts are compressed into murmurs and JPEGs. In this environment distributed material is planted in a user's cache, a fragment of an idea. To borrow from Umberto Eco's conception of the 'anti-library', this form of dissemination might present glimpses of the unknown and trigger the desire to discover and unpack the potential imagined therein. Independent publishing's ace card is the visible, unread book.

AND
Eva Weinmayr

The Piracy Project
The definition of artistic activity occurs 'first of all in the field of distribution' replied Marcel Broodthaers when asked by fellow artist Herbert Distel to contribute to his *Museum of Drawers* back in the '70s. Broodthaers refused. This is raising an old question: whether artwork locked in a drawer is still a work of art. Is the fact that a work is perceived and seen by others a vital condition of its existence? I think yes. Books, for instance, need a reader. They won't wake up and play unless they are animated, responded to and appropriated by an imaginative mind.

Taking things further, some readers even start to 'love books actively' — words used by writer Jonathan Safran Foer to describe his appropriation of the translated novel *Street of Crocodiles* by Polish author Bruno Schulz, in which he cuts out individual words, thereby producing a new work.

Could this compulsion be shared by the book pirates, who anonymously added two extra chapters to the version of a Jaime Bayly novel, sold in the streets of Lima, Peru in 2010? Skillfully written, these chapters remain indistinguishable from the rest for the unprepared reader. What is

Call for Contributions

The Piracy Project is not about stealing or forgery. It is about creating a platform to innovatively explore the spectrum of copying, re-editing, translating, paraphrasing, imitating, re-organising, manipulating of already existing works. Here creativity is not in the borrowed material itself, but in the way it is handled.

www.andpublishing.org

crucial however is that whereas Safran Foer puts his own name onto the book cover, the pirates in Lima remain anonymous. They purely infiltrate other authors' books as a playground for their own imagination.

In a similar vein *The Piracy Project* that we started in London last year, collects publications not conventionally authored but enriched, improved, reviewed and appropriated in many different ways. The works in the Piracy Collection are self-consciously and freely borrowing the authority of other authors, their canon or context, to make their own points. Fundamental questions around the relationship between authorship and ownership are implicitly raised.

Throughout the project we travelled to Istanbul, Lima, New York, Berlin, Shanghai and Beijing to research cultural piracy in different settings and discovered various innovative approaches to the re-contextualisation of creative works. In a striking example, a book in Istanbul has been published and authored by more than 120 individuals in an act of solidarity with the author, whose unpublished manuscript landed him in prison before it could be officially published. Even though he is still imprisoned, the book circulates. The dispersal of authorship becomes a tool for free speech.

Importantly, *The Piracy Project* also showed us that not only artists and writers, but also publishers, programmers, academics, business people and architects have started to challenge existing structures. Questioning issues of authority as well as ways of producing and redistributing cultural products and values, these 'pirates' have taken matters into their own hands. Our platform is constantly evolving.

Banner Repeater

Un-Publish

The railways witnessed Britain's transformation from an agricultural to an industrial economy, as the increased efficiency demanded by the rapid developments in trade and labour during this period thoroughly homogenised time.

Publishing, distribution, dissemination; the sharing of ideas, filter bubbles that then isolate us from each other again, the speeds of data we receive warping our sense of time and attention, speak of our now, very everyday, post-industrial time.

Click-drifting through 'locust swarms of lettering' described by Walter Benjamin almost a century ago, as writing was 'ruthlessly dragged out into the street by advertisements and subjected to the brutal heteronomies of economic chaos': the maze of digital code we inhabit, for all intents and purposes, means that we can type a lot better.

The representational map that presented what was out there, for us to use for our own devices, (albeit drawn for someone else's), has become an interlaced web, daily inscribed by every transaction we perform, make public, or perhaps detrimentally publish, within this heavily mediated networked space, while algorithms; the 'filters' that drive our desires, customise our experience.

The recent and increasingly exposed construction of consensus, arising from a bias in spectacular news reporting: an oversimplified 'victims-and-aggressor' meme, flocking from one focus of this sort to another, (and not unique to the tabloids, by any means) performs a particularly consistent form of reality management whose efficiency is enabled, all the more so by the tools of citizen journalism.

Ideas regarding technology, open-ness and democracy proposed by the networked structures of web 2.0, ignore for the most part the materiality of digital data and its supporting frameworks, and do not necessitate emancipatory projects in and of themselves, but are tools that provide new methods of communication that also impact upon our sense of a collective and political voice. The technology that facilitates the vast consumerism of capitalism, is at some core level, implicit also in our ability to act politically, and affects our understanding of what it is to be politically engaged, certainly with respect to older hierarchical structures and former traditions that may come into question as a result.

'Un-publishing' (Julian Assange) accounts for the condition whereby online data is particularly susceptible to tampering, in that it is exceptionally easy to delete. No trace is left of it ever having been there. You would have had to know it was there in the first place. Contrary to what we may suspect, traditional print media has a potentially longer shelf life, through the wide distribution of material: paper, that resists the censorious reach of corporations and authorities, (increasingly colluding), whether commercially or politically motivated.

The archive of artists' published material at Banner Repeater, sites this resource in the lives of commuters, passing through a working station environment during peak travel times. Multiple points of dissemination, both on-line and via the

inter-connected transport networks that platform 1, Hackney Downs rail station is enmeshed in, distribute these works throughout the city and further afield.

Book Works

Why distribute?
The first part of this question is seemingly quite simple, and follows on from an earlier question, *Why publish?* when we asked fourteen publishers / artists / art organisations, including ourselves, in Book Works' publication *Put About: A Critical Anthology on Independent Publishing* (edited by Maria Fusco with Ian Hunt, 2004) to provide some responses in the context of their own practice. Seven years later we asked another similar-sized group to contribute to this publication, by asking the questions *Why distribute?* and *Why archive?*

As a publisher, the answer to the question 'why distribute?' seems superficially obvious, for without a readership there seems little or no point to producing books.

However, more than that, distribution is a two-way activity, one in which we can actively engage in sharing information, ideas and networks, as well as identifying an audience with similar interests. It's about taking risks, putting something out there for people to react to, interact with etc., and by 'making public' to provide that link between the artist / author and the reader who completes the process of book publishing. In relation to *Again, A Time Machine* I like the idea of the backward / forward space that artists' books might occupy, sitting on a shelf, they re-emerge at different points: in a second-hand bookshop, in a library, under a pile of other books, in a skip, taking on a different readings as each year passes — unfashionable, fashionable,

unread, important, obsolete … … … as Karl Holmqvist's contribution to *Make the Living Look Dead* aptly describes, REWRITE, in which the letters form a circle, with no beginning or end.

Why archive?
Like the White Columns *UPDATE* exhibition catalogues (shown on pp. 135–36), there is something satisfying about trying to give an overview of a moment in time / group of artists etc., and a sense of history, or personal achievement. Yet perversely, with *Again, A Time Machine*, we found ourselves more drawn towards both commissioning new work that dealt with the back / forward issues of time and archives as seen, for example, in the project by Slavs and Tatars' *Dear 1979, Meet 1989*, and presenting *Make the Living Look Dead*, a semi-fictitious exhibition of artists' works, that would then self-consciously become part of our official archive. Ephemera, small jokes, messages, propositions and reflections — this is the stuff to which we are often drawn when picking through collections, especially with the easy access to digital information for more formal research material.

Our history is both incomplete and expansive, and as much to do with the history of process, instincts and desires, as an accumulation of objects and finished works. When visiting Paul Buck's house (an archive in flux) while we were editing his book *A Public Intimacy (a life through scrapbooks)*, it was his idiosyncratic cataloguing system — a letter from Kathy Acker, 'filed' in between the pages of one of her books, a whole section on crime writing, French philosophical texts, a drum kit etc., that sparked off the

KH 2011

connections and provoked new ideas, that juxtaposition of moments of weight and levity that convey the value of the archive.

Eastside Projects

The following text is comprised of six modified entries and two new entries from the *Eastside Projects User's Manual*.

ACCUMULATING

At the end of each exhibition at Eastside Projects we build on, recycle and up-cycle its remains. In this way, each exhibition alters the space, and the space constructs an archive of its production and evolution. Each new addition responds to and alters the existing conditions. The gallery accumulates the traces of its use as part of a learning process. See also TRANSFORMING (*Eastside Projects User's Manual Draft 5*, freely available from Eastside Projects).

ARCHIVING

We archive as an active process of forming the gallery. As such our archive is partial and unstable. Archiving may not be the best method of reflecting on or supporting art production. Archiving may be unnecessary. See also MYTH-MAKING.

DISTRIBUTING

A proposition: distribution is the means by which messages go out into the world; the actions that are prompted by sharing information, knowledge, ideas, and conditions. We distribute to subject our output to the forces imposed on them by circulation. We distribute to participate in other systems: in search of criticism, to improve our environment, as a marker, as experience. Distributing is necessary. See also PUBLISHING.

DOCUMENTING

Artist Stuart Whipps has been making photographic documentation of activities at Eastside Projects from a series of fixed positions since before the gallery opened in 2008. In May 2011 Whipps installed eight camera mounting brackets in new fixed positions around the gallery. Periodically, during 'Narrative Show' (May to September 2011), the artist made new photographs from these positions, recording the transformations occurring in the space. See also ACCUMULATING.

DOG-WHISTLING

As a contribution to the exhibition 'This is the Gallery and the Gallery is Many Things' (September to November 2008), Kelly Large instigated a perverse social ritual in the gallery. Each morning, following the opening of the building, the alarm was left to sound until a passer-by or neighbour entered the building to complain. This process forced our immediate neighbours — a taxi repair workshop and a limousine hire company — to enter the gallery, where they were prompted to look around. Large likens this process to a dog-whistle, suggesting that Eastside Projects' most receptive audience is remote — outside Birmingham — and encouraging us to continue to foster local relations, to make our distribution act at various registers. See also DISTRIBUTING.

MYTH-MAKING

The world is understood through myths. All meaning comes to us as stories. We can take control of these stories to create our own meaning and form new myths. Fragments of stories and half-remembered truths form constantly re-written histories and articulate new and possible futures. See also RETAINING.

PUBLISHING

We publish to produce a mobile aspect of the gallery space. We produce printed matter, books, billboards, comics and editioned artworks. See also DOG-WHISTLING.

RETAINING

We have a developing policy to negotiate with artists commissioned to make major works for Eastside Projects, to retain a copy of any edition as a legacy gift to a future Birmingham Museum of Contemporary Art. See also ARCHIVING.

Mark Pawson

Why distribute?

Whilst thinking about what I wanted to say in this article I realised that I've distributed my own and other people's work since I was sixteen and at school in a small Cheshire town. In 1980 I was selling trapezoidal envelopes and spray-painted postcards for 8p each in the corridor outside the sixth-form common room. Simultaneously I was sending Postal Orders off to Better Badges in London, buying piles of fanzines and selling them on to friends, without taking a profit. I wanted to get my own work out there and into other people's hands, making it available at affordable prices and also to share the new, exciting world of independent publications, which I'd discovered via mail order.

Today I continue to sell my own work, alongside a personal selection of work from other small independent publishers that is unavailable elsewhere in the UK, at book fairs and through a website, as well as distributing wholesale to a few independent retailers. My activity as a distributor has developed and grown, becoming more defined and focused, but I feel that the reasons I do this remain very close to the original impetus that got me started in the 1980s.

Why distribute?

• To make some money to pay for your next book.
• To make some money to buy goat cheese and pesto tortellini from Sainsbury's.
• To make some money to pay the rent.
• To make some money.

Why archive?

In 1985 I did some research at the Tate Gallery Library for my thesis on Mail Art. I was pleased to gain entry to this resource and thankful to have access to a wide range of obscure publications unavailable elsewhere.

In 1986 I stayed in Graf Haufen's West Berlin apartment. One wall of the tall, thin living room I slept in was dominated by shelves of box files, their looming presence felt foreboding. My instinctive response was to make a drawing of the shelves, adding an elaborate funeral urn on the top shelf and to leave this drawing for Haufen to discover after I'd left Berlin.

In 1989 I undertook some recreational research into Eduardo Paolozzi's Krazy Kat Arkive at the Victoria & Albert Museum Archives, looking at some of his vast hoard of toys, model kits, knick-knacks and ephemera.

In 1994 I bought twenty Fellowes corrugated cardboard file boxes. I felt ambivalent about spending money on storage materials

instead of making work, but it seemed like some books and magazines had formed into groups and now demanded recognition and protection. Here are some of the file box names: VILEs, Schmucks, Smiles, Lightworks, Ross Martin, Subgenius, Schwa, Le Dernier Cri and Stuff I Sold.

In 1999 I had an edition of 200 'No New Work' archive boxes custom-made by W. MacCarthy & Sons Ltd. Made from 2mm thick board and measuring 8 x 27 x 34 cm, they're designed to be both practical, for housing collections of my work and also as vanity objects, as a way of creating my place on library shelves and in archives. They were sold either empty or pre-filled with an instant collection of Pawson Products.

After moving house in 2007, I purchased a Big Dug industrial shelving unit which measures 89 x 135 x 179 cm and now contains lots and lots of boxes of STUFF, and my bed is on top. I'm avoiding the term 'Archive' here, preferring to regard it all as a slightly haphazard, ad hoc accumulation of things. Swivelling round I can see the labels on some boxes, I'll let you have a peek: Mailart — Early, Ecart, Tuli Kupferberg, Austin / Playbitch, Anti-Media, AAA, LPA, OMRLP, DWMAC, My Thesis, A5 Pamphlets …, Zines etc. …, 1980s FANZINES, Copy Culture, Artists Books info / Catalogues, Robin Crozier, Found

Magazine, Stewart Home, Neoist Alliance, Even more Gonks & Noggins, Shelves in front room #14, Monkeys ++++, Pez, Mr Potato Head + Kinders + Candy Containers + Walkers.

In October 2008, I made an edition of Perspex signs with the slogan 'NEVER THROW ANYTHING AWAY EVER'.

In 2011, I received two requests to loan material for exhibitions, they were time-consuming to deal with properly, but worthwhile. Even more unexpected was the donation / repatriation of a box of 1980s mail art from a friend who was dispersing his archive. So now, after thirty years of collecting, non-disposal and just stashing stuff in A4 paper boxes, this agglomeration of publications, correspondence, rubber stamps, small plastic toys, etc., etc., has coalesced into an Archive. It seems like this Archive has somehow activated itself, with the recent loan requests acting as a curatorial catalyst.

Pil and Galia Kollectiv

Retroviral distribution

In the introduction to *Grundrisse*, Karl Marx objects to the simplistic historical idea that the process of production has to precede distribution in an economy. Even the straightforward distribution of commodities is trickier than it initially seems: to produce something necessitates the availability, and therefore distribution, of tools of production. Even agricultural production is based on the distribution of its basic unit of productivity — land. In short, production and distribution are (as are exchange and consumption) fused together in a dialectical unity, flowing in a 'movement which relates them to one another, makes them appear indispensable to one another, but still leaves them external to each other'. In this text, Marx is not interested in merely pointing out the false methodology of classical economics. His real target here is the humanist assumption that underlies liberal economic thinking, that a human being, fully capable of rational decisions, exists prior to the process of socialisation via work. Subjects do not exist in the abstract space that precedes an economic, social or a historical reality: they produce their environment through labour and are at the same time produced by it. Post-Fordist forms of labour have added more weight to this argument. Symbolic, cultural and real capital are produced today directly from distribution (of knowledge, images, stock, tastes and opinions etc.) Re-tweeting, re-blogging, 'liking', sharing and so forth, are all mechanisms of value production that are purely distributive and the more information travels the network the more it is productive. The actual production of this information requires only a bare minimum of authorship, with random images and ideas only commodified at the point of distribution.

Within this landscape, the answer to the question of whether it is desirable to distribute cultural products becomes a lot less self-evident. Since content is an emergent, secondary factor in this economy of value, cultural production becomes highly co-optable. Any desire to undermine or disrupt this system instantly turns into yet more fodder for user-generated content platforms and other forms of investment in the self, with the aim of appreciating the value of one's human capital. In other words, distributing your ideas is good for enhancing your CV, but in an economy where your portfolio of activities, thoughts and tastes are your biggest asset, it's hard for those ideas to retain any subversive intentions targeting this economy. In light of this problem, you might understandably choose to withdraw from the incessant flow of communication and information, and indeed, there has been a spate of philosophical suggestions of exodus and abstention in post-Autonomist thinking, from Virno to Bifo to Agamben. But like the outsider artist whose work is 'discovered' and absorbed into the canon posthumously, you cannot outrun the exponential reach of viral distribution. Resistance, it seems, is futile.

However, if distribution is an inevitable fact of our networked existence, it's worth considering subspecies of viruses that might function slightly differently with regards to the contagious spread of information.

Retroviruses like HIV alter the DNA of their hosts as they infect them in a reverse transcription of the genetic code. Without adhering too strictly to the scientific account of these organisms, we would like to think about this operation in relation to distribution as cultural production. The first example that comes to mind is Guy Debord's *Mémoires*. In 1957, Debord published his collage of newspaper cutouts, splatter painting by Asger Jorn, photos, cartoons and architectural plans bound in a heavy sandpaper cover. Its aim: to destroy any books placed on a shelf next to it. As Greil Marcus notes in his book *Lipstick Traces*, this strategy was later adopted by The Durutti Column, who similarly sandwiched their debut album, *The Return of the Durutti Column*, between two sheets of sandpaper, dutifully glued on at a very reasonable piece rate by a broke Joy Division as they watched porn VHS tapes in the Factory Records flat.

The second example is the NSK passport, issued by the Slovenian art group's 'state in time'. This a-territorial convincing looking document famously helped refugees from war-torn Yugoslavia cross borders at a time when NSK was as plausible a name for a new state as any of the myriad emerging nation states of the region. More recently, when thousands of Nigerians started acquiring these artworks, occasionally under the false impression that they granted entry to Slovenia, the Slovenian government has actually had to issue a statement explaining the status of NSK as an art project. It is these forms of retro-virally infectious distribution that we need to learn from if we want to intervene in the cycles of cultural valorisation generated by the current regime.

Publish And Be Damned

Hey Kate and Kit, *Why distribute?*, *Why archive?* Why don't we try to write something together? I love a bit of dialogue. If it's slightly tongue in cheek, and not too conceited, we can get across the collaborative nature of PABD, and present ourselves as more than one voice and so seem inclusive and un-didactic and avoid pinning down exactly who or what we are, which is always a good position to be in. I was thinking I could reference what Michael Warner writes about in *Public and Counterpublic* — what he said about gossip and a public being 'a relation among strangers' seems relevant to both archive and distribution, and to us having a conversation. Why don't we write it out on paper and scan it like we normally do for our invitations? I like the way crappy handwriting can become a trademark. Actually, I hate it. I don't want Publish And Be Damned to become a brand, an umbrella organisation or a Eurotrash Printed Matter Incorporated. Why do we shy away from becoming professional? Because we are lazy? Or because we need to occupy the space between the artist, the hobbyist and the fan? Is this an attempt to resist something? I don't want to get slick, but I do want us to do more and to do what we do better. Perhaps this earnestness is something to do with being a fan. We talked a lot and decided we wouldn't become a distributor of self-publishers, but of course in aiming to promote our members, our job is distribution. Or is it dissemination? Dissemination implies something more haphazard, more scattergun (I want to insert the word squirt somewhere here) than the measured control of distribution. Warner says 'the address of public speech is both personal and impersonal … To address a public, we don't go around saying the same thing to all these people. We say it in a venue of indefinite address and hope that people will find themselves in it.' Distribution aims for certain customers and audiences, certain readerships … Publishing, making public, should also involve being found, involve talking to people you do not know. Warner argues that gossip, because of its circulation and lack of control, appears perfectly public, but is never 'a relation among strangers'. It's never impersonal — 'You gossip about particular people and to particular people.' So gossiping is not making public, even though it is. And diary writing and love letters aren't either, even though they can become so, if they are well written enough to be of interest to someone else. Mail Art is publishing only in a similar archival manner

— it presumes that it will be stored — that one day someone will want to gather it. As publishing it is vain: it fails in its attempt to reach strangers and it's arrogant — presuming a future readership. We still describe the fair as for 'self-publishers', even though one of our 'rules' is not to include publishers who only self-promote. We avoid the vanity press, while wholeheartedly embracing the alternative it offers. We need people to come to our fairs and discover something new in a mass of stuff. We need them to feel like they have eavesdropped into a conversation that is interesting, even though they have no idea what it is about. Like The Archive (with an upper case T and A) we need to avoid making too many spurious claims about being democratic, un-curated and un-edited. We need to lose 127 words. Kit, you said you could reel off something for Jane really quickly, so we have a back-up plan, but either way I hope you'll agree that the last thing we need is a manifesto. The last thing anyone wants is a monologue.
Lou x

Spike Island
Marie-Anne McQuay

'How not to distribute?' is one possible rejoinder to the question 'Why distribute?', if we equate with self-publishing the information shared through our habitual voluntary and involuntary on-line actions. Conjured up by searches and transactions, the animated sizzling fly-size commercials that plague Chic, the protagonist of Philip K Dick's *Simulacra*, have found us at last, nearly fifty years later.[1] Additionally, the multiple virtual forums for personal updates and pronouncements, along with platforms designed for lengthier and worthier disseminations, allow for a continuous merging of self-mediation and self-distribution. Given that it has never been easier to be seen and heard in the twenty-first century, the Internet has consequently become the graveyard of our good intentions, literary and otherwise, a rhizomatic monument to half-finished projects that still promise to emerge as a particular form of future past (*Coming Soon*, 2006).[2] That is not to say distinctions between print and digital, publishing and transmitting, do not exist, nor, crucially, matter; rather that they are perhaps more pronounced for those of us for who the pleasures and frustrations of last century's analogue limits was lived experience instead of a borrowed aesthetic manifested in faux-flickering footage and simulated Polaroid tones.

The Internet is also an archive of sorts, albeit a decentred site via which we upload images and text, indexing the present and constructing an understanding of the past. When writing of the photograph's mimetic potential, Baudelaire proposes that this new form of documentation rescues, 'from oblivion those trembling ruins, those books, prints and manuscripts which time is devouring, precious things whose form is dissolving and which demand a place in the archives of our memory'.[3] And so it is that distributed visual and textual information, now divorced from the materiality of paper and silvered copper plates, is our own mnemonic legacy, yet a potentially unstable and impermanent one, equally capable of dissolving, part of what Benjamin, the collector's collector, the preserver of his own archive, described in another era as 'the struggle against dispersion'.[4] Since the corporate database and file servers that host and co-own our content are expensive to maintain and have no contractual obligation to preserve over the long term, when combined with our own inability to create individually-held systematised data as we migrate from device to device, what appears to be a permanent record is just a temporal illusion. When such systems fail us, as they inevitably will, we will be pieced together instead from traditional archival sources, from medical, educational, financial and governmental records, as well as

the faint traces of life-long on-line habits. Thus if self-publishing as self-mediation is now both a casual and inevitable act, then perhaps archiving should be reconsidered as a conscious and deliberate strategy, a necessity re-learnt to counter the narratives that would otherwise describe us only through our civic records and data trails.

1   Philip K. Dick, *The Simulacra*, Gollancz, Orion Publishing Group, London, 2004. 'Something sizzled to the right of him. A commercial, made by Theodorus Nitz, the worst house of all, had attached itself to his car. "Get off," he warned it. But the commercial, well-adhered, began to crawl, buffeted by the wind, towards the door and the entrance crack. It would soon have squeezed in and would be haranguing him in the cranky, garbagey fashion of the Nitz advertisements.'
2   Nicolas Bourriaud, *Factor 2000*, FACT (Foundation for Art & Creative Technology), Liverpool, 2002. 'Make sure you are seen and heart in the 21st century', Bourriaud uses this phrase to describe the Superchannel, an early video webcasting project set up by Superflex in 1998 which predates Youtube, with its analogous slogan 'Broadcast Yourself', by seven years.
3   From *Archives, Documentation, and Institutions of Social Memory: Essays from the Sawyer Seminar*, ed. Francis X Blouin Jr and William G. Rosenberg, The University of Michigan Press, 2010. From 'Records of Simple Truth and Precision: Photography, Archives and the Illusion of Control', Joan M Schwartz .
4   *Walter Benjamin's Archive: Images, Texts, Signs*, Verso, London, 2007.

The Serving Library
Stuart Bailey, Angie Keefer, David Reinfurt

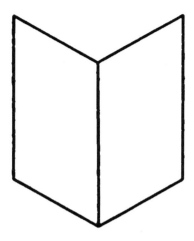

The following paragraphs have been pulled from the distributing archive http://www.servinglibrary.com/

HERE IS A THOUGHT-EXPERIMENT. Imagine yourself in a virtual space surrounded by icons: a familiar optical illusion that looks like an open book projecting first out then in then out again; a claustrophobic negative photo of a woman, apparently underwater; a large asterisk; another open book in a heraldic shield, underscored by the phrase 'Lux et Veritas' — Light and Truth; a man blowing what appears to be a handful of feathers but turns out to be a disintegrating book; a curious-looking alien glyph; and an odometer on the brink of changing from 9 9 9 9 9 9 9 back to zero.

These are the front pages of a number of Portable Document Formats, and this is http://www.servinglibrary.org/, engine room of The Serving Library. Each PDF is a 'bulletin' containing an article or essay that constitutes part of some overarching theme or themes — in this case, from specific to general: Libraries, Media, and Time. The essay behind the large asterisk, for example, contemplates the possibilities for human communication in light of some extraordinary physical attributes of the Octopus Vulgaris. As it turns out, that 'asterisk' is actually *an octopus in plan view.* This and the other PDFs are available for anyone to download for free. Contributions to the latest theme are added from time to time over a six-month period, and at the end of the season they are collected together into a single document, printed and published in both Europe and the USA, each in an edition of 1,500, as *Bulletins of The Serving Library*. The PDFs remain available on the website, while a new theme is developed over the next half year.

One copy of *Bulletins of The Serving Library* is bound in hardback leatherette, catalogued, and placed on a shelf in the physical home of The Serving Library. Here it joins past issues, along with twenty issues of its predecessor, the left-field arts journal *Dot Dot Dot*. A neighbouring shelf carries a larger collection of older, most frequently referenced books by the circle of contributors to both *Dot Dot Dot* and the *Bulletins* — on art, literature, philosophy, and so on — that maps a far-reaching but still very particular constellation of interests. And on another shelf is a further assortment of relatively recent titles covering a wide gamut of contemporary publishing that had been sold from — and often published by — Dexter Sinister, a design workshop and bookstore on Manhattan's Lower East Side that was run as a primitive form of The Serving Library by two of its founders from 2006 to 2011.

The first libraries were premised on an archive model, where important documents were held in restricted strongholds, eventually supplemented by a circulating model, where resources were pooled for collective use. The ecology described here amounts to a further development, the distributing model, which combines and extends the first two. Publishing and archiving have traditionally existed at opposite ends of the trajectory of knowledge production, but here, in accord with the cheap and easy distribution afforded by an electronic network, they coalesce into a single process. In this way The Serving Library diagrams a reversible, looping principle: it is an archive that publishes and a publisher that archives according to a motto borrowed from the annals of library science: HOSPITIUM AD INFINITUM, or infinite hospitality.

The Showroom
Emily Pethick

While The Showroom has accumulated a linear archive of its activities over the last 26 years, it is one that lies low. We have, however, been involved in the development of a number of archives through our work with artists. With a focus on collaborative and process-driven practices, open-ended forms of production, and forms of artistic research, a number of our projects have involved distributed archives and archival practices.

For example, for over two years we have been working with Lawrence Abu Hamdan on his *Aural Contract Audio Archive*, which looks at the politics of listening and the role of the voice in law, employing a range of research methods, including seminars, workshops with young people, and interviews. Containing audio extracts of his work, along with examples of juridical listening and speaking gathered from a wide range of sources, it includes the trials of Saddam Hussein and Judas Priest, UK police evidence tapes, films, and readings from texts, including Italo Calvino's *A King Listens*. Taken collectively, the material radically opens up ways of understanding the power of the voice, and how it is heard.

The Brussels-based organisation Agency is constituted by an ongoing list of 'Things' that resist easy categorisation. These include divisions between nature and culture, creations and facts, subjects and objects, humans and non-humans, individuals and collectives, and are derived from judicial processes, lawsuits and cases, controversies or affairs around intellectual

property. At The Showroom, Agency posed the question of 'how to include collectives in art?', looking at how the law struggles to define collaborative relationships when problems arise. Objects and materials associated with particular cases were exhibited alongside case notes, and an Assembly was held in which a diverse group of 'concerned guests' — each of whom had a different expertise in relation to it, including a drummer, a composer, a writer and legal expert — was invited to discuss one particular case.

Cinenova: Reproductive Labour brought the films that are distributed by the womens' film distributor Cinenova and their archive of paper materials to the gallery. This enabled material that in the past has been difficult to access to be made openly available and explored through events and discussions that were held around particular films. The exhibition created the platform for important and difficult questions to be raised in relation to Cinenova's past and future, including its positioning and sustainability and the labour involved in maintaining it, and for these issues to be public, and socialised. The Cinenova Working Group, which organised the exhibition, was present during opening hours, mediating the work for visitors, and at the same time starting to digitise the collection.

Cinenova was founded at a time when women film-makers had little visibility, a problem that they tried to address through strength in numbers. Archives are intrinsically collective, and in many cases are as much constituted by the knowledge they produce, and the people that surround them, as the material they may or may not contain, and thus can hold multiple viewpoints and inherent conflicts and contradictions in tension. In the cases illustrated here, archival practices become specialised sites of critical enquiry through which questions can be asked that can challenge how knowledge is produced and categorised, and who has access to it. They can be activated and distributed, and through movement, gain from local knowledge, remaining in process, and continually in question.

Torpedo

Independent publishing as an autonomous field often ascribes to the idea of art as communication. The relationship between art and publishing is even thought of as reaching an apex within this particular idea of art as communication, with a genesis in the historical avant-garde, prolonged by the Fluxus movement and expressed through artists such as Joseph Beuys and his statement that 'everyone is an artist'.

If the primary task is to make art communicate, the highly regarded freedom and autonomy of independent publishing should be taken with a pinch of salt. The idea of art as a direct link between the author / subject and public was not just put under pressure by the neo-avant-garde, but was the origin of how new concepts of art could be spread and distributed in differing social contexts, as was the case with the use of printed matter in the 1960s and 1970s. That is a question that is usually glossed over, even today: what role does the book play after production, the receiver, the reader, or what if it never reaches a reader at all? Distribution often takes place outside of the more common distribution systems and is seldom part of a library's stock or a bookstore selection.

Whereas curators and institutions publish books en masse and there is an increase in the number of artists who experiment with the book as a format and employ it as part of their artistic practice, technology allows for publishing through web portals and social media. There's a thin line between publishing content online and publishing by print on demand. Why publish books when everyone can be a publisher on their own blog? After all, what still fascinates about the book and printed matter as an art form is how it relates to an egalitarian tradition of utopian communities within art, where hierarchies can be broken down and the exclusivity of the art object is averted with the possibilities that technology of mass production and distribution offers.

In Thomas Pynchon's *The Crying of Lot 49* the main character, Oedipa Maas, gets wind of a secret post service of unknown origin, and it turns out it has a hidden history that can be traced through nursery rhymes, tagging, engineering patents and a baroque tragic drama. What initially seems like fleeting signs and observations, is made manifest as a competing postal service named Tristero. As a parallel system of communication, mainly used by entities that no longer conform to society's raison d'être, Tristero functions like a denial or negation of the official postal service.

An opportunity to name the rules and construct and organise viable systems outside of formal and institutional structures is a history that DIY publishing shares with other counter-culture movements. But just as the postal service in Pynchon's novel is subject to antagonism that manipulates, turns and undermines it, independent publishing could also be seen as a viable strategy to resolve the validity of these structures with whims, coincidences and interpretative errors, rather than producing an alternative (any alternative).

Ubuweb
Kenneth Goldsmith

Archiving is the new folk art, something that is widely practised and has unconsciously become integrated into a great many people's lives, potentially transforming a necessity into a work of art. Now, at first thought it seems wrong: how can the storing and categorising of digital (or analogue) data be folk art? Isn't folk art the opposite, something predicated upon the subjective handcrafting of an object into a unique and personal statement, often times one that expresses a larger community ethos? One need think only of, say, the magnificent quilts of Gees Bend produced over many generations by a group of African-American women who live in an isolated Alabama town. Each quilt is unique, while bearing the mark of that specific community. Or the spectacular cosmic visions of someone like Rev. Howard Finster, whose obsessive, emotional hand-rendered religious paintings and sculptures could only have sprung from the unique genius of Finster himself.

Like quilting, archiving employs the obsessive stitching together of many small pieces into a larger vision, a personal attempt at ordering a chaotic world. It's not such a big leap from the quilt maker to the stamp collector or book collector. Walter Benjamin, an obsessive collector himself, wrote about the close connection between collecting and making in his essay 'Unpacking My Library': 'Among children, collecting is only one process of renewal; other processes are the painting of objects, the cutting out of figures, the application of decals — the whole range of childlike modes of acquisition, from touching things to giving them names.' In Benjaminian terms, all of these impulses — making, collecting and archiving — can be construed as folk practices.

Let's add to that the organising of digital materials. The advent of digital culture has turned each one of us into an unwitting archivist. I spend much more time acquiring, cataloguing and archiving my artefacts these days than I do actually engaging with them. The ways in which culture is distributed and archived has become profoundly more intriguing than the cultural artefact itself. What we've experienced is an inversion of consumption, one in which we've come to engage in a more profound way with the acts of acquisition over that which we are acquiring; we've come to prefer the bottles to the wine.

Our primary impulse, then, has moved from creators to collectors and archivists, proving Benjamin, once more, to be prophetic: 'If my experience may serve as evidence, a man is more likely to return a borrowed book upon occasion than to read it. And the non-reading of books, you will object, should be characteristic of collectors? This is news to me, you may say. It is not news at all. Experts will bear me out when I say that it is the oldest thing in the world. Suffice it to quote the answer that Anatole France gave to a philistine who admired his library and then finished with the standard question, "And you have read all these books, Monsieur France?" "Not one-tenth of them. I don't suppose you use your Sèvres china every day?"'

White Columns

The W.C. #20 (Volume 2, number 8)

Update
Published on the occasion of the exhibition *Update*, 3 April to 2 May 2008, featuring work by 11 artists who had exhibitions in White Columns' recent past: Anthony Campuzano, Carter, Jennifer Cohen, Peter Gallo, Tamar Halpern, Colter Jacobsen, Lars Laumann, Sarah Anne Lobb, Mitzi Pederson, Eileen Quinlan, John Stezaker.

Xerox publication, 28 pages, staple bound, 11" (h) x 8 1/2" (w)
OUT OF PRINT

The W.C. #35 (Volume 3, number 11)

Update #2
Published on the occasion of the exhibition *Update #2*, 15 March to 16 April 2011, featuring work by 11 artists who had exhibitions in White Columns' recent past: Violette Alby, Mark Barrow, Steven Baldi, Josh Brand, Patricia Esquivias, Judy Linn, Marlo Pascual, Noam Rappaport, Josh Shaddock, Alexandre Singh, Jennifer West.

Xerox publication, 24 pages, staple bound, 11" (h) x 8 1/2" (w)

update

update

update

update

update

update

update

update

update

update #2
update #2
update #2
update #2
update #2
update #2
update #2
update #2
update #2

X Marks the Bökship
Eleanor Vonne Brown

It's summer 2011 and I am in Arnaud Desjardin's studio on Occupation Road rummaging through boxes, searching for gems in folders stuffed with exhibition invites, catalogues and a various assortment of printed material. Everything from a Focal Point Gallery poster of last month's show to some fading ephemera from the '60s and '70s. I'm really curious about all this folded paper with black type from other times and places produced by people I've never heard of. He keeps pulling things out, unfolding them and each one's got a story to go with it. One of the stapled booklets that catches my eye is a dealer's catalogue from Backworks, a bookshop in New York that was run in the late '70s by a woman called Barbara Moore. It's a list of all the books in stock with prices and sometimes a cover photograph. Her partner Jon Hendricks was a photographer who would document all the books they distributed and the events they hosted and vigorously archive them and then produce occasional black and white newsprint catalogues that they would circulate to collectors and anyone who was interested in artists' publications. On the cover of the issue I'm holding is the strapline 'Was Ist Backworks?' What is Backworks? I think. How have I never heard of this place with all these books and all these happenings? But that is the nature of these types of ephemeral places that come and go with limited lifespans burning as long as the energy of the people who run them lasts. That evening I go home and begin a list of all the books I have in stock at the Bökship. Pages of titles of short-run publications by independent publishers. I put the list on my website and I also print it out and photocopy it onto a few pages that I staple together and give to Arnaud next time I see him, for him to add to one of his piles of paper that hopefully one day someone will discover, unfold and have a glimpse of what was happening in London in 2011 / 2012 during this wave of independent artist publishing.

NOTE

THIS big new presentment of a little old story is of course for the sake of Mr. Sheringham's illustrations. I might, perhaps, in revising now the proofs of what I wrote so long ago, have been tempted to alter drastically this and that passage; but it struck me that if at the time when I wrote it I had caught an elderly and pedantic stranger in the act of tampering with my MS. I should have been enraged, and rightly enraged. So I have forborne to tamper. But I reflected also that if, soon after the story was first published, this stranger had with his gnarled and tremulous forefinger pointed out to me certain printers' (let us say printers') errors that I had overlooked, and even had he in the fullness of his experience ventured a hint on punctuation here and there, I might have felt rather grateful to him. So I have not scrupled to correct some mis-spellings and transpose some commas.

M. B.

Rapallo
1915

THE HAPPY HYPOCRITE

BY MAX BEERBOHM

ILLUSTRATED BY GEORGE SHERINGHAM

LONDON
JOHN LANE, THE BODLEY HEAD
NEW YORK: THE JOHN LANE COMPANY

George Sheringham 1914

"KING BOGEY"

Commissioned to host *The Happy Hypocrite* readings, Eastside Projects, 31.3.11; Spike Island, 8.10.11; The Showroom, 2.6.12; and participated in a performance event at Motto/Chert, 13.5.11.

Notes on three happy hypocrites

Maria Fusco

I am glad I never saw his Lordship. They say he was rather like Caligula, with a dash of Sir John Falstaff, and that sometimes on wintry mornings in St. James's Street young children would hush their prattle and cling in disconsolate terror to their nurses' skirts, as they saw him come (that vast and fearful gentleman!) with the east wind ruffling the rotund surface of his beaver, fur about his neck and wrists, and striking the purple complexion of his cheeks to a still deeper purple. 'King Bogey' they called him in the nurseries.

There are three happy hypocrites in this essay. The first, chronologically to state the obvious and to say the least, is English essayist Max Beerbohm's short story 'The Happy Hypocrite', first published in 1897, a tale marked by the moral preoccupations and formal language of its time. The second, *The Happy Hypocrite*, is a semi-annual journal for and about experimental art writing, founded by myself in 2008, marked by the authorial anxieties and resourceful syntax of our time. The third, the happy hypocrite (please note three typographic shifts in our obliging term) is a methodology, a way of working, a citizenry of non-division.

Deep down among the weeds and water lillies of the little stone-rimmed pond he had looked down upon, lay the marble faun, as he had fallen. Of all the sins of his Lordship's life surely not one was more wanton than his neglect of Follard Chase. Some whispered (nor did he ever trouble to deny) that he had won it by foul means, by loaded dice.

What is it to write today? Thinking through now: to enact fascination in the world through perceptual subjectivity; to be concerned with precision of delivery through textual method; to aspire to contribute to the production and distribution of knowledge. Who owns this knowledge once it has been published? Pause: as a cognitive device, writing may be a trail, both for the one who has written it, and for those who subsequently read it, determining its own critical criteria in each new context through usage. In this way there can be no summative ownership, merely formative tenancy.

" DEEP DOWN AMONG THE WEEDS AND
WATER-LILIES LAY THE MARBLE FAUN "

"HE STOOD ON THE BRIM OF GARBLE'S
LAKE. SHOULD HE DROWN HIMSELF?"

He stood on the brim of Garbel's lake, shallow and artificial as his past life had been. Two swans slept on its surface. The moon shone strangely upon their white, twisted necks. Should he drown himself? There was no one in the garden to prevent him, and in the morning they would find him floating there, one of the noblest of love's victims. The garden would be closed in the evening. There would be no performance in the little theatre. It might be that Jenny Mere would mourn him.

Hard to tell what will be decided in advance, intentions are bleak without results. Impossible to tell what has already been decided, the reader shapes the writing.

It was a bright morning in Old Bond Street, and the fat little Mr. Aeneas, the fashionable mask-maker, was sunning himself at the door of his shop. His window was lined as usual with all kinds of masks.

This pressing desire for movement, this necessity to share more easily, more practically, more generously, than through talk alone. Which tools might work best to achieve this aim? Publishing? Once a book or journal is published its contents may not be easily amended, at least without having being noticed first. I write: Corrigenda are not incorrigible. I like the way these four words sound on the page. Deceleration, through publishing, is dictated by and owes its efficiency to the shared responsibilities of its contributors, its editors and its publisher: at this stage, the reader is without mote. Publishing, as this pressing desire to experiment in public may, if it is agile, cause disarray of discipline through a willingness to accept messiness as method.

"HIS WINDOW WAS LINED AS USUAL
WITH ALL KINDS OF MASKS"

"THE DISGUISE WAS DONE"

So soon as he was sure of its perfect adhesion, he took from his assistant's hand a silver file and little wooden spatula, with which he proceeded to pare down the edge of the mask, where it joined the neck and ears. At length, all traces of the 'join' were obliterated. It remained only to arrange the curls of the lordly wig over the waxen brow. The disguise was done. When Lord George looked through the eyelets of his mask into the mirror that was placed in his hand, he saw a face that was saintly, itself a mirror of true love. How wonderful it was! He felt his past was a dream.

Corrigenda are not incorrigible.

He, who had done no good to human creature, would pass unmourned out of memory. The clubs, doubtless, would laugh and puzzle over his strange recantations, envious of whomever he had enriched.

The archive is an uncertain motor for production, in that it instructs and demonstrates all the reasons why you should not go on. I read something excellent. I cannot go on. I read something awful. I cannot go on. To investigate and acknowledge relevant archives is sensible, for of course it's neither pleasing nor wise to proceed without first acquiring substantive research, but such archival research is beleaguered with diversions, bolted gates and stiles which are best treated with balletic amnesia, in order to go on.

'THE CLUBS, DOUBTLESS, WOULD
LAUGH AND PUZZLE OVER HIS
STRANGE RECANTATIONS"

Swift as a kitten, Jenny chased the buns, as they rolled, hither and thither, over the grass, catching them deftly with her hand. Then she came back, flushed and merry under her tumbled hair, with her arm full of buns. She began to put them back in the paper bag. 'Dear husband,' she said, looking down to him, 'Why do not you too smile at my folly? Your grave face rebukes me. Smile, or I shall think I vex you. Please smile a little.' But the mask could not smile, of course.

The absurd is a special kind of material playfulness, ontological in interest, solipsistic in nature. It is repressed through repetition; singular instances of the absurd in form are preferable then, speaking to choice above peer pressure, hanging amidst a temporary absence of feeling, so worry can't creep in. Here the individual voice is encouraged, snubbing simulated relation through location to instigate change. Smart as a paper cut.

JENNY WITH HER ARM FULL OF BUNS

"OH, SHE IS COMING IN!"

'Oh, she is coming in!' George heard the latch of the gate jar.
'Forbid her to come in!' whispered Jenny, 'I am afraid!'

The italicised text in this essay are quotations extracted from the 1915 edition of *The Happy Hypocrite*, accompanied by George Sheringham's original illustrations.

A pro bono practice
Barry Sykes

Hello. My Name is Barry Sykes and I'm an artist, works on paper, ad-hoc sculptures, process-based interventions, that sort of thing. And my reading today is entitled 'An Apology, An Excuse, An Explanation'.

I'd first like to say thank you to Marie-Anne McQuay of Spike Island, Maria Fusco of 'The Happy Hypocrite' and Book Works for the opportunity to do this.

Maybe I should start with the apology. I don't think I'm really meant to be up here. I've not published anything; I'm not working with any of the publishers present today. I haven't made an artist's book for years. To be quite honest I don't even read books that often. I'm just a visitor but have somehow made it up on stage.

Let me briefly explain how I think this happened. About a month ago I saw an advert for a paid role asking people to sit in this gallery reading out loud from a new book of short stories by Dora García as part of this current exhibition 'Again, A Time Machine'. Knowing I was going to be in Bristol this weekend to attend the fair I applied to take part then thought no more about it. When I got a confirmation email a few weeks later saying I was all booked in for the event today I admit I skimmed the rest of the details.

Then, when the email reminder came through a few days ago -- and I read all of this one -- it immediately became clear what had happened. As is no doubt evident to you all, today those reading have been replaced with a different proposition; for contributors to the fair to read out from their own publications, this time without a fee, to be recorded for Spike Island and 'The Happy Hypocrite' -- as the invite said, 'To deliver a short essay, ideally your own'.

So, I guess my excuse for being up here, is that through the generosity of the curators, unbeknownst to me, I've been allowed to sidestep into this opportunity to contribute alongside the others.

Now, I've written and delivered a number of presentations in recent years, many of which I could have just used for today. There's one about my personal finances, one about pretending to work as a part-time policeman, one about a planetarium, one about always being mistaken for someone else, one was the imaginary transcript of an unmade film of a monologue delivered on a nudist beach, one was a set of questions about how to really fail on an artist's residency, and many years ago I even read out an little known J. G. Ballard short story surrounded by ten taxidermised polar bears right here in this gallery.

But all those were ideally written or recited for a specific moment, they don't really have a link to what's going on here today and besides they're all much too long for the ten minutes we've each been allotted onstage today. So I've had to come up with something new.

Of course when I realised what was expected of me I could have just said, 'Oh, my mistake, I didn't realise that was the deal, I'm not sure I've got anything appropriate' but I knew I didn't want to turn down the chance to do something for Spike Island or Book Works. So the only option was to use the last few days to come up with something completely from scratch. Which might make my text the newest, or the least thought out. In fact if I stumble at all it's because I may be reading my edits and annotations from the margins.

So, all the speakers are providing content, to be recorded, so it must have some quantifiable value. But as I said before, as far as I know, today's readings are delivered by us all without payment or artist's fee. We all knew this and have gladly taken part.

For a while now I've had an idea, or tactic, that I've wanted to try out and perhaps this is the best place to launch it. As I'm sure many of you will recognise, it's often the case that as an artist you want to contribute something but there is no fee. You are quite free to walk away but your curiosity or ambition won't let you. I should say that I know Book Works and Spike Island in particular are both dedicated to supporting artists' ideas and careers and to be quite honest they're both organisations I'd like to work with in the future, I know they're trying to do the most with the money they have. And of course it was my choice to write something completely new -- the classic over-delivering artist. In fact I think the decision to contribute or not is one of the important freedoms you have as an artist. It is your right to decide yourself whether you do or you don't take part, but also your responsibility.

So, here's my tactic, let me explain. Every time I willingly accept an invitation to provide some sort of content for a project (be it text, documentation, or a concrete object, any activity) where some people are being paid but I am not, let's say for organisations with a reasonable turnover, funding, or more than one paid employee; every time I decide I can shoulder the time, energy and expense myself and still give it my all, I will call it my 'pro bono' work.

Just as an architect, accountant or lawyer might offer to undertake certain projects for cash-strapped organisations for no fee, because they decide they want to give something back, they can just about afford it, it makes them feel good and it looks good for their reputation, I will do the same. Pro bono, from the Latin 'pro bono publico' or 'for the public good', defined as 'professional work undertaken voluntarily and without payment or at a reduced fee as a public service'.

From now on I will list these projects on my CV and website as normal but next to them will be the two words 'pro bono', a proud declaration that they were performed under these circumstances. If you yourselves are artists then no doubt you have also willingly accepted these types of offers in the past, I'm sure with all the enthusiasm and energy you would for the times when you're paid for your work, but how to tell them apart? When I list today under my talks and presentations I will label it pro bono, as I now will for every other project under similar conditions. If you want, please feel free to do so too.

Thank you.

PRO BONO POSTSCRIPT

On the day, my presentation got a slightly nervous reaction from the audience. A few gasps and chuckles of recognition in the right places and happily a number of people coming up to me afterwards saying they knew exactly what I was talking about. The organisers seemed awkwardly appreciative, one even jokingly pressing a ten pound note into my hand, which of course I refused as that kind of fund-raising was not my objective. Sometime afterwards I received an email from Book Works that began 'Hello Barry ... we really liked your work and wanted to ask if you'd be willing to let us republish the text in a book we are working on that documents and extends the 'Again, A Time Machine' exhibition ...' Fantastic! 'We can't offer a fee but ...' Riiight.

Now, based on the stance outlined in my presentation I couldn't really let that go unquestioned, so felt empowered to ask Book Works a series of questions about why there was no fee and on the financial situation of the whole publication, to which they kindly provided frank and thorough answers; in short, there are small fees for the main contributors, none for brief pieces like mine and a very modest budget for the entire project. Of course I'm aware Book Works are a non-profit organisation, running on limited resources, in a tough climate for the arts, but as that is the case for the whole of the non-commercial artworld in the UK should that really rule out the chance of earning a living, even pocket money, for your efforts? My concern is how all these arts organisations

are trying to generate as much output as possible with even more modest means and the buck often stopping with the plucky, ambitious artist
eager for exposure and willing to take the delayed gratification. And I
feel like every time someone accepts or doesn't feel they can question
conditions such as these it gets much harder for anyone else to expect
any better, and gives no encouragement to arts organisations to make a
change. So what am I doing still contributing? Well, if I'm honest, I'm
as conflicted by the pay-offs between exposure, enthusiasm, in-kind support and cold, hard cash as the next artist. On balance I was convinced
I should say yes and take the hit twice, as alongside respecting Book
Works and liking the project as a whole, I'd crucially been allowed to
put my case across. Am I right? Am I wrong? Maybe you have an opinion?
Needless to say, this contribution will also unfortunately have to be
designated pro bono. Ah well.

Lancaster Castle
15ᵗʰ Septʳ 1862

The County of Lancaster
To William Clemusson

Preparing & erecting scaffold for
the Execution of Walter Moore   £2 . 9 . 0
3 men 3½ days each @ 4/8 per day

Erecting Scaffold during the Night   1 . 1 . 0
Grave & 4 Carriers   — . 15 . 0
                                  £ 4 . 5 . 0

allowed   JWManisty

16ᵗʰ Septʳ 1862
Recᵈ payment
William Clemusson

Memo. paid in 1857. £3. 6. 6
       paid in 1858. 3. 15 —
       paid for Watchers £6. 6. 0

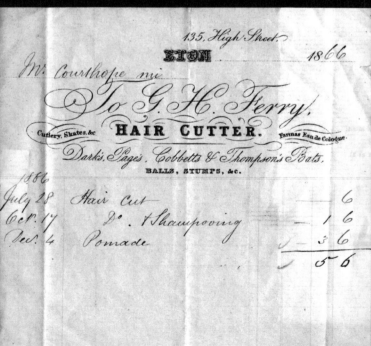

135, High Street.
ETON   1866
Mʳ Courthope ⁿⁱ
          To G. H. Ferry,
Cutlery, Skates, &c   HAIR CUTTER.   Farinas Eau de Cologne.
     Dark's, Page's, Cobbett's & Thompson's Bats.
              BALLS, STUMPS, &c.

1866
July 28   Hair Cut   6
Ocʳ 17   Dᵒ & Shampooing   —   1   6
Decʳ 4   Pomade   √ — 3   6
                                   √   5   6

Commissioned essay following contribution to *Existential Territories*, Book Works, 17.7.10; and the publication by *Mute* of *Dear Living Person* and *Dear Living Person: The Story of the Eyes*, 2011.

Autonomy is not worth the paper it is not written on: Writing. Written. Art-writing. Art. Writing.

John Russell

I have in my hand two photocopies: please take into account that these examples of writing have more impact and charisma in their 'original' distressed and elegantly inked format.[1] The first is a copy of an invoice for the cost of the execution of one Walter Moore in 1862. Inscribed in flowing script and addressed to William Cleminson, at the County of Lancaster, Lancaster Castle, on 15 September 1862, it details as follows:

> Purchasing and erecting scaffold for the execution of Walter Moore
> 3 men, 3 ¼ days each @ 4/8 per day — £2. 9s. od
> Erecting scaffold during the night — £1. 1s. od
> Grave and 4 carriers — 15s. od
> Total cost — £4. 5s. od

The other document is the bill for the haircut of an Etonian schoolboy at T.G.H. Ferry Haircutters, 135 High Street, affixed to an itemisation of the essential yearly expenses of an Eton student, both dated 1866. The bill for the haircut is handwritten on a printed bill, as follows:

> Haircut — 6d.
> Shampooing — 1s. 6d.
> Pomade — 3s. 6d.
> Total cost — 5s. 6d.

1 x haircut = 1/16th of an execution. I have no knowledge of Walter Moore: neither of his class nor occupation, nor the nature of his crime; nor indeed any idea of which Etonian schoolboy was getting a haircut. For the time being it is enough to remind ourselves that these are *both examples of writing*. And here is another:

> Above this eruptive cadaver, the head, tumultuous, enormous, encircled by a
> disordered crown of thorns, hung down lifeless. One lacklustre eye half opened

---

1   The original documents reside in the collections of the
    Centre for Ephemera Study, Department of Typography
    and Communication Design, University of Reading.

as a shudder of terror or of sorrow traversed the expiring figure. The face was furrowed, the brow seamed, the cheeks blanched; all the drooping features wept, while the mouth, unnerved, its under jaw racked by tetanic contractions, laughed atrociously.

Huysmans, *La Bas*, 1891.

And one final example:

PARTICULARS RELATED TO THE INFORMATION NOT CONTAINED HEREIN CONSTITUTE THE FORM OF THIS ACTION.

Christine Kozlov, 1970.

All of these are examples of writing. The last is an example of writing that is also art. And the second an example which is also literature. They are all also examples of surface. Both in the way that a page / paper / screen / text is a *surface* — in the way *this page* is a surface. And the way that my 'skin' (or your skin) is a surface — with its foul lubrications — presented to the world, albeit mainly hidden from view. And also in terms of the cross-articulation of different types, categories, registers and intensities of surface: the surface of meaning, the surface of ideas, the surface of politics, the surface of art, the surface of objects, the surfacing of sense, the surface of dead people, and so on. As Rancière writes: '… the relations between the surface of the exhibition of forms and the surface of the inscription of words.'[2] But this might also include the relation between 'the surface of inscription of words' and the shiny surface of a kidney dialysis machine, the casing of a land mine, moonlight reflecting on a lake, or the shine of tears in the eyes of a young child.

Christine Kozlov's 'text' — writing which is also art — was a telegram sent to Kynaston McShine, curator of *Information*, 1970 and operates as a negation of representational information as the mode of its representation (and / or a parody of this). Echoing the negative dialectics of Duchamp and Broodthaers, where the negation of the status of 'art' operates as the articulation of that status.[3] The Kozlov text is also an art-historical example of the turn to language of the 1960s / 1970s which is often characterised through its relationship to philosophy (in particular Anglo-American philosophy of language) as mimicry of this scientific style.[4] This 'turn' also included the co-opting of the critical (and articulating) force of art's 'support languages' (criticism, theory, curation) to create new formats of production that were immediately assimilated as institutional genre, including: 'conceptual art', 'critical art' and 'institutional critique'. And as experimentation with the potential of text / language as 'printed matter', able in its ubiquity to move across the boundaries of art and non-art and 'high' and 'low'. For example Dan Graham's *Homes for America* (1966 / 1967) and other magazine works, released into the freedoms of extra-institutional 'chaos', only to be reclaimed by institutional mechanisms (as above). In contrast, the contemporary language turn of *art-writing* (it is claimed) orientates itself in relation to literature and fiction. A quick survey of recent debates regarding 'art-writing' suggests the influential writers may include Acker, Joyce, Beckett, Sebald, Bataille, Ballard, Perec, Borges, Johnson, Tillman, Burroughs, concrete poetry, magic realism … (the usual suspects).[5] As Tom McCarthy proposes, 'in the current climate UK publishing is a very conservative field … art has become the place where literary ideas are received, debated and creatively transformed'. John Douglas Millar puts another spin on this, suggesting: 'art-wrting' is '… a phenomenon or a construct formulated to justify academic funding and careers' adding 'the art world is a place where a bad writer can hide', a place where '… books are the final ruins of modernity, a Tintern Abbey for the digital age' and ends up suggesting there's no such thing as art-writing but only 'writing without boundaries'.[6] *L'écriture sans frontières* as the trivial illusion of freedom, glimpsed through the prison bars of category. Not so much a dream as a curse, rotting out of the stinking corpses of literature and art. The degraded conservatism of 'literature' mirroring the degraded conservatism of 'art' — two stinking corpses. As the crowd screams in Stewart Home's spoken word polemic '… We want books full of sex, violence and anarcho-sadism, not boring literary shit in which nothing happens',[7] synchronising with his descriptions of art in *Defiant Pose*,

> The trouble had spread down Millbank and word had just reached those at the epicentre of the disturbances that the Tate Gallery had been fired. The news that billions of pounds' worth of modern art was going up in smoke brought loud cheers from the crowd. […] To achieve freedom they had to erase, demolish and otherwise destroy the very architecture around which the bourgeoisie had engineered the domination of their class. The city would have to burn and burn and burn before this destructive frenzy reached its orgasmic resolution! Watching the Houses of Parliament reduced to a smouldering ruin made Terry and Joyce feel horny as hell.[8]

In his famous essay of 1979, Lyotard describes how knowledge is transformed into 'information', legitimated not in relation to abstract principles — 'metanarratives' — but in terms of performative effectivity, that is, standardised relative to the efficiency with which

2   Jacques Rancière, *The Future of the Image*, Verson, London and New York, p. 79.

3   The validation of *Fountain*, 1917, as 'Art' was dependent on the judgement by the selection committee (Society of Independent Artists) that it was 'in no way art'. Replayed (after Magritte) in Broodthaers's use of the label 'This is not art' placed by objects in the exhibition *The Eagle from the Oligocene to the Present*, at the Kunsthalle in Düsseldorf, 1972, requiring the viewer to have already translated the object as the statement 'This is Art' for the second statement to make sense.

4   In his influential essay 'Art After Philosophy', 1969, Kosuth tries to portray his own position as more conceptually extreme and philosophically rigorous than other artists contemporaneously described as conceptual by claiming the legacy of Wittgenstein. But this tendency was not influential among many of the other artists conventionally associated with conceptual art, for instance Smithson, Weiner, LeWitt, Graham etc.

5   This list is compiled unscientifically from suggestions made in John Douglas Millar, 'Yes But is it edible?', *Art Monthly*, no. 349, pp. 11–14; the responses to this article by Gavin Everall, Maria Fusco and Sean Ashton in *Art Monthly*, nos. 350, 351 and 352, 2011; and Dieter Roelstraete, 'Word Play', *Frieze*, no. 139, May 2011.

6   Ibid., pp. 13–14.

7   Stewart Home, 'From New Britain', from *Cyber-Sadism Live!*, Sabotage Editions, London, 1995.

8   Stewart Home, *Defiant Pose*, Peter Owen, London, 1991, pp. 131–32.

it achieves prescribed outcomes (echoing Frankfurt School / Habermas's descriptions of the domination of social, political, and economic life by the goals of logic and efficiency).[9] If you think this through with reference to Foucault's ideas of discourse, as a structuring of power which determines who may speak the truth and where / when they may speak it, then this points to a system where it doesn't matter what is said (or written) but rather who says it (writes it) and where it is said (or written).[10] Negri and Hardt elaborate on these ideas in their descriptions of the 'informatisation' of production and the domination of the informational economy.[11] To paraphrase Foucault, the meaning of any particular instance of the use or performance of language is much less important than the fact of its emergence or articulation.[12] That is, the articulating force of language as something that does rather than says — as that which either does (or doesn't) emerge through / in the articulating structures of power. This is what we marvel at in the art world: the magic of emergence and articulation — as fact. As we stand there joyfully blinking at the miraculous FACT of arrival. Of the presentation of the 'given' and given-ness as profound and divine. And as proof of our own worthiness as spectators, heralded by (the second coming of) Duchamp's ready-made in the 1960s, which moves the focus from the object to our acknowledgement of its arrival / articulation (as art). De Duve suggests this twists Kant's aesthetic judgement from 'This is beautiful', to 'This is art'.[13] The pure categorical imperative of social relations, 'I think this is art therefore everyone else should think this is art' translated through the 'free-play' of market forces and social relations in the coming of art as 'given'. As a fact, or ontology. This is the transformation of art's conservatism into a kind of 'beauty'.

Unlike (for instance) *Who wants to be a millionaire* or *The X factor* where there is still the degraded requirement for a question to be answered or a song to be sung (as a kind of 'phantom-limb' protocol), art experiments with a more radical dialectics of use and exchange value. More radical dematerialisations and capitalisations, where anything can stand in as a marker for 'art' and anything can be paid for.[14] This is the prophecy of 'free play' already described by Marx in his analysis of commodity form where the worker sees their social relations transformed into the social relations of (commodity) objects. The transformation of dumb objects into social objects as a demonic animation of dead things.[15] Where an ordinary table evolves 'out of its wooden brain grotesque ideas, far more wonderful than "table turning".'[16] And so art becomes a celebration of these invisible articulating forces as DIVINE — as the power which bestows the magnificent gifts of visibility subject to its own unknowable calculations. And these bestowments validated as proof of this divinity, in the ecstatic moment of articulation and given-ness.

In this context, language (or writing) should not be considered as a system of communication, either inside or outside the institutions of art / literature, but of ordering and fixing. If language operates performatively (in the way described above) then the meaning is irrelevant. Only the force is relevant. Or at least the force is the meaning. Power is meaning.

How therefore … does 'art-writing', 'text-based' art or 'book art' operate within these languages of articulation, given that these are activities also concerned with 'using language'?

One answer is to *say exactly the same as everything else* — as any other object — or art object. How could they 'operate' differently? A book will, if successfully entered within the networks of the art institution, perform in the same way as any other object, picture, sculpture, piece of string, kangaroo, idea, film etc. It will, or will not, generate within us the same 'thrill' of recognition of arrival. The thrill of the fact of its successful articulation as art (or not).

I guess we should say at this point — at the very least — that there is no such thing as art-writing or writing without boundaries — only writing (as articulated). Writing in Chains. Obviously.

But yes … yes … some people would argue that this is an overly reductive description. It could be argued that — even if we accept this account of articulating / interpolating forces — that a book is an unusual type of object. And all that has been described so far is the performance of a book or text in as much as it is an art object or any other kind of object, articulated by the structures of discourse. But a book is also … a book. An object made up of paper with words on them.[17] What if the language in / on the pages has nothing to do with the 'language' by which the book is articulated as an artwork, or anything else. What if there are different types of language, different qualities and intensities, even if we accept this overarching context of articulation. Perhaps when the book is being read, we are removed from the influence of the other kinds of language. The language 'inside' a book might be different. Like the succulent contents of a guava fruit — a rich area inaccessible to 'information'. A kind of change of speed / attitude / pitch or whatever that puts it out of the reach of the rest of culture, or at least these interpolating forces. Like the soft innards of this vermin …

And with that she grabbed the crow and squeezed its body — the bird squawking and pecking at her fingers — until its innards squeezed out of its mouth.

Helen was talking without moving her lips. She continued: 'But this is just the familiar claim that has been trotted out for the arts regularly throughout history. The idea that there are different levels and qualities of production, in art, literature, music, cinema, that suggests liberation or sanctuary from the fascistic propagandas and languages of an otherwise instrumentalised mass culture. The same old high / low, elite / mass distinction that is used whenever art or literature wants to distinguish itself from everything else. To distinguish its "depths" from other types of surface … and surfacing …'

9   Jean-François Lyotard, 'The Postmodern Condition', 1979, in *The Postmodern Condition: A Report on Knowledge*, Manchester University Press, Manchester, 1984.

10 For instance *The Order of Things: An Archaeology of the Human Sciences*, 1966, Tavistock, London, 1974. Or *The Archaeology of Knowledge and the Discourse on Language*, 1968, Pantheon Books, New York, 1972.

11 Michael Hardt and Antonio Negri, *Empire*, Harvard University Press, Cambridge, 2000.

12 Michel Foucault, *The Archaeology of Knowledge*, p. 100.

13 Thierry De Duve, *Kant After Duchamp*, MIT Press, MA and London, 1997, p.453.

14 Having said that, it could be argued that the recent sale of 'high-yield', 'speculative' or 'junk' bonds — the sale of debt — is creative and experimental in a more radical way than art's quaint dematerialisations.

15 Marx describes commodities as possessed by the Devil. Karl Marx, *Capital*, vol. 1, Penguin Books, 1990, p. 302.

16 Ibid., p. 163.

17 'Book' (as a metaphor) and this would include e-books, PDFs, blogs, smoke signals, Morse code etc.

Helen looked down at her hand, smeared in the shiny wet blood of the crow. '... and here the object-ness of a "book" is configured as a skull, or ribcage, or church, or sanctuary, a casing of book cover and pages shielding the precious interior (content, poetry, criticality) from the ravages of totalitarian philistinism. Protecting one sort of "language" as the "rich" textuality of depth, from the outside, as the impoverished superficiality of surface.' As Heather Love writes:

> There is perhaps no term that carries more value in the humanities than 'rich'. In literary studies especially, richness is an undisputed — if largely uninterrogated — good; it signifies qualities associated with the complexity and polyvalence of texts and with the warmth and depth of experience.[18]

Through the lens of this 'depth hermeneutics'[19] other forms of cultural activity — the usual suspects — certain types of TV, Hollywood cinema, popular music — are characterised as 'thin and dead' (surfaces).[20] 'Depth' is opposed to 'surface'. The spectacularised imagery (of capitalism) slipping across the dead and thin surfaces of popular culture like the projected light of a TV nature documentary sliding across the greasy meat of a McDonald's burger. But the twist here is that these surfaces are deceptive — they are / must be. They must be powerful / forceful, to enable the logic of the Mass Culture argument. Flat and dead maybe, but not weak. For instance the shallow (meaningless) but forceful rhetoric of politicians, or the manipulative language of advertising. As in Deleuze's analysis of 'sense',[21] where language is configured as surface affect, as for instance performed in a judge's pronouncement that condemns a man to execution on the gallows.[22] The judge's sentence is neither complex, nor content-full, nor beautiful, nor 'deep', but nonetheless transforms the meaning of the convict's body on the level of flesh, not present 'in' the body, but articulated with the breaking of necks. The same language that writes the construction of a gallows or an expensive haircut abstracted in the equivalence of exchange value. Language can therefore be performed as either 'shallow', thin, meaningless and powerful (forceful), or deep, rich, meaningful and powerless (impotent). Autonomy and complexity can only be preserved as a kind of withdrawal. As a glimpse of freedom. According to this logic.

If the turn to language in the 1960s / 1970s might be seen as a response to art's own 'depth hermeneutics', as an attempt to take control of the critical forces (languages) that 'explain' and validate art as art, and to confront art's own traditional anti-intellectual (bourgeois) mysticism, where art is 'beyond' history and language, then the current fashion for art-writing and the criticism of art-writing (and the debates around the *crisis in criticism*), restage this hollow opposition. As the opposition between language-as-meaning or language-as-beyond-language-as-non-meaning-as-meaning.[23] Both positions attempting to preserve the weak freedoms of 'subjectivity', 'agency', 'autonomy', 'complexity' or 'politicality' through allegiance to either the rigours of 'clarity' and the precision of words / language as communicating knowable knowledge, or to the intuitions of a lack of clarity and the imprecision of words/language as non-meaning as unknowable knowledge. Two claims, echoing ancient refrains: form/content, text/image, aesthetics/content — either writing should make sense, or that it should not. 'Pingu does criticality' or 'Pingu does poetry'. And this also includes familiar hybrids, such as the self-reflexive strategies so beloved of the art institution, that retain the 'agency' of the autonomous, author figure, as a subjectivity acting out the agency of being self aware of its own lack of agency, while simultaneously gesturing a comedy shit-finger at the baroque graveyards of institutionalised criticality (as a foregrounding of self awareness). Criticality. Post-criticality. Institutional critique. Post-institutional critique and so on. And the audience are all dead … corpses — we are the audience, lined up in the comfy seats staring blankly at the screen, our heads full of shit and straw. The problem with this is that writing — all writing — will inevitably make sense, how can it not? However the words are organised. However critically, clinically, scientifically — or poetically, absurdly, randomly. But they will make the same sense every time. As Derrida describes this: '… we can pronounce not a single destructive proposition which has not already had to slip into the form, the logic, and the implicit postulations of precisely what it seeks to contest'.[24]

It was clear Helen was getting angry. For a few seconds she couldn't tell if Rodrego was still there. He seemed distant. Seemed to be fading away. She continued: 'Rather than re-rehearsing fantasies of escape, what if we try to think through how text/language/publications might operate not as separate from but as a continuation, or intensification of, the meaningless/forceful language of information/articulation, that we anyway-always have to act/write within. What about, for instance, if "autonomy" is not worth the paper it is not written on.'

A little badger had climbed over the wall. His fur was thick with soot. As he scrambled up the last section of brickwork he heard Helen's words and it seemed the ideas struck a note. He responded to her point excitedly: '… "autonomy" … not worth the paper it is not written on … ? Intensification … ? Very interesting. How might that work?'

18 Heather Love, 'Close but not Deep: Literary Ethics and the Descriptive Turn', *New Literary History*, vol. 41, no. 2, Johns Hopkins University Press, Spring 2010, p. 371.

19 Heather Love describes how social scientists Bruno Latour and Erving Goffman have little time for the 'traditional humanist categories' of experience, consciousness, and wish to replace 'depth hermeneutics', with descriptions of surfaces, operations, and interactions'. Heather Love, op. cit., p. 376.

20 '… from the fat and living to the thin and dead', from Erving Goffman, 'Role Distance', *Encounters: Two Studies in the Sociology of Interaction*, Bobbs-Merrill, Indianapolis, 1961, pp. 83–152.

21 Deleuze describes the [incorporeal] sense [of the event] as: 'an incorporeal, complex and irreducible entity, at the surface of things, a pure event which inheres or subsists in the proposition.' Like 'The sun is shining' expresses a sense that 'inheres' in the proposition, but is never reducible to the state of affairs of either one specific or even an endless series of specific instances of a shining sun — but at the same time, in each case, is imminent to its SPECIFIC/PARTICULAR expression. Gilles Deleuze, *The Logic of Sense*, Columbia University Press, New York, 1990, p. 19.

22 Gilles Deleuze and Félix Guattari, *A Thousand Plateaus: Capitalism and Schizophrenia*, Continuum, London and New York, 2004, p. 89.

23 See Maria Fusco et al., 'Eleven Statements Around Art Writing', *Frieze Blog*, 10 October, 2011, and Dan Fox's response — available at http://blog.frieze.com/11-statements-around-art-writing/ — or any of the countless 'crisis in criticism' symposiums/conferences at an art centre near you.

24 Jacques Derrida, 'Structure, Sign and Play in the Discourse of the Human Sciences', 1967, in *Writing and Difference*, University of Chicago Press, Chicago, 1978, pp. 280–81.

The badger sat on the wall, his wet nose twitching expectantly. But it seemed that in front of him there were two dead bodies propped up in chairs and that behind them the rest of the restaurant had been blasted away. A wreck of chairs and smashed glass. Bloody bodies and limbs strewn throughout the carnage. A bomb blast.

Helen continued: 'For instance the example of *Reena Spaulings*. This is a book … initially written as a *kind* of art book, or a book that was a kind of art work … narrating the story of a kind of artist called Reena Spaulings … articulated (in the book) by the structuring of the art world, moving from her job as a gallery guard to fashion model, and meeting Žižek in a bar … kind of slacker sub Dennis Cooper Brett Easton Ellis style. Although not so many people have actually read the whole book, many people have read the first few chapters online, or at least have a general idea of what the book is about, and what it does. The book was presented among other things as a 'book as artwork' (possibly written by multiple authors) … but it was also presented as other things — as a novel, a gallery, an artist,[25] … and as a kind of fraud … which is to say a kind of 'fictioning' and/or most importantly as a kind of prophecy.[26] As a prophecy of the successful articulation of the book as a kind of artwork and/or gallery. Now the book has almost entirely become a gallery — a successful gallery, with artists and exhibitions — which also works as a kind of story. To quote John Kelsey (one of the gallery directors and authors of the book): "In Miami the first thing we sold was a painting by Merlin Carpenter — a blank white canvas splattered with the words DIE COLLECTOR SCUM, in black. The next work we sold was a ready-made garbage can by Claire Fontaine."[27] This is still part of the "story" of *Reena Spaulings*, as a gallery which exists both inside and outside "quotation marks". And as a book, "containing" a fiction, and as a fiction itself, which "fictions" the performative/information flows inside and outside of the book — as both "language as fiction" and "language as articulation".'

She coughed out blood onto her hand. Her face white. White. This wasn't the time or place to be talking about art-writing. But she persisted: 'We can extend this by proposing that writing might be considered in relation to the idea of the "Hack", which, as John Kelsey has suggested, involves an "attempt to engage (and perform) the problem of the hack-writer's own participation within (and extension of) the networked communicational space they share with art" and further to this, to be "… immediately involved in the question of how to elaborate (habitual) rhythms of production today … getting closer to a possible and paradoxical definition of art through assuming art's increasing loss of distinction from other communicative activities". And then if we consider the idea that "… the hack is one who starts from no distance. He begins from his own commodification, from the fact of being for hire … The hack is always there — always in play".'[28]

The criticism of Kelsey's position would be that either 'Hack writing' is so close to 'real' hack writing as to be indistinguishable from the 'history-free debate' and 'marketable psychobabble' of the 'complementary inflight magazines' of the art world.[29] Or otherwise the claim has to be made for a subversive, political role or attitude for this position of adjacency that also includes some way of distinguishing it from all the things it is adjacent (close) to but isn't. Which is the same old curse of 'reporting back' — creeping back into the gallery with a special kind of 'art-hack-writing' for the consumption of sophisticated cultural connoisseurs.

But Kelsey's text is also reminiscent of Walter Benjamin's analysis when he writes in 'Writer as Producer':

> Rather than asking, 'What is the attitude of a work to the relations of production of its time?' I would like to ask, 'What is its position in them?' This question directly concerns the function the work has within the literary relations of production of its time. It is concerned, in other words, directly with the literary technique of works.[30]

Technique is the keyword here. A call for the development of writing defined according to the development of techniques that produce a transformation of its forms — in the same way that technology produces a transformation in the way we live our lives. Since 'technique' is a productive force, then, literature can be read as occurring in tandem with the conditions of production prevailing at any given time (which includes reproduction / mediation and transformed post-Fordist informatisational modes). Although we have to be careful here to avoid the pitfalls of McLuhanesque technological determinism, 'the medium … shapes and controls the scale and form of human association and action',[31] technological religiosity, a 'semi-religious faith in the inevitability of progress […] a kind of invisible hand guides technology ever onward and upward …'[32] or technological fetishism, as Head Gallery writes:

> He spent hours running his fingers over the cold metal of the factory cast machinery, thrusting his strap-on through any aperture he could find. The obdurate rigidity summoning up and re-embodying the flavours of years of servitude and enslavement. The smell of metal. The close-up of distressed paint and serial numbers. He could smell the hundreds of years of clock in / clock out drudgery. And when he licked the metal, he could taste it. The abstraction of labour time

25 Reena Spaulings: 'The One and Only', Hauswellediger & Co Gallery, New York, 2005; *Reena Spaulings*, Semiotext(e), New York, 2005; Reena Spaulings, 165 East Broadway, New York.

26 'I am well aware that I have never written anything but fictions. I do not mean to say, however, that truth is therefore absent. It seems to me that the possibility exists for fiction to function in truth, for a fictional discourse to induce effects of truth, and for bringing it about that a true discourse engenders or manufactures something that does not as yet exist, that is, "fictions" it.' Michel Foucault, *Power / Knowledge: Selected Interviews and Other Writings 1972–1977*, ed. Colin Gordon, Pantheon, New York, 1980, p. 93.

27 John Kelsey, 'The Hack', in Daniel Birnbaum and Isabelle Graw (eds.), *Canvases and Careers Today: Criticism and Its Markets*, Sternberg Press, Berlin and New York, 2008, p. 66.

28 Kelsey, op. cit., p. 67.

29 Merlin Carpenter, 'The Tail That Wags The Dog', 2007, in Daniel Birnbaum and Isabelle Graw, op. cit., quoted here from http://www.merlincarpenter.com/tail.htm.

30 Walter Benjamin, 'Author as Producer', in *Selected Writings, vol. 2: 1927–1934*, Harvard University Press, Cambridge, MA and London, 1999, p. 770.

31 Marshall McLuhan, *Understanding Media*, Mentor, New York, 1964, p. 9.

32 Carroll Pursell, *White Heat: People and Technology*, University of California Press, Berkeley and Los Angeles, 1994, p. 38.

congealing in his mind. He even felt a strange stirring in his loins when he was running his cheek over the metal of these machines. A kind of eroticism — the eroticism of oppression. He began to fellatio levers.[33]

In the background, ambulance crews begin to pick their way through the debris. Through the upturned tables and shattered brickwork and bloody bodies. Stopping here and there to check for signs of life. A woman is screaming. Lying on the floor, her legs blown off. She is screaming in a foreign language.

The badger has a strange pained expression on his face, reminiscent Helen thinks, of the expression on the face of her father on that evening when he was told he had cancer. The badger interrupts her memory with his high-pitched insistent voice: '… perhaps the only real art-writing or art book is the instruction manual for photo manipulation software. Or perhaps a funding application — could this qualify as authentic art-writing? Or a CV. A press release?'

And Helen had to admit this was an interesting proposition. It is indeed difficult to distinguish one sort of writing from another. To decide when one sort of writing ends and another sort starts? This might be to do with an appreciation of the ending of one sort of game and the starting of another with a new set of rules? But what if we take Benjamin seriously for a second when he writes that 'only one demand' imposes itself upon the writer, the 'demand to think, to reflect on his position in the process of production' (A similar starting point to Kelsey). And then: '… only by transcending the specialisation in the process of intellectual production — a specialisation that, in the bourgeois view, constitutes its order — can one make this production politically useful; and the barriers imposed by specialisation must be breached jointly by the productive forces that they were set up to divide. The author as producer discovers — even as he discovers his solidarity with the proletariat — his solidarity with certain other producers who earlier seemed scarcely to concern him.'[34]

And this might include solidarity with other surfaces — not just human ones — in the breaching of specialisation. And also including humans as surfaces, or as shapes or trajectories of mammal meat. As a contemporary opening up of the techniques of writing onto the surfaces of production and/or transforming modes of production and processes of articulation (which are also surfaces), including pre-programming of our expectations of future 'transformations' and so on. The same modes of production which should be in public ownership but aren't. The same modes of production we can't escape.

Not as re-performance of pre-existing roles performed differently (as in Butler), or camouflage or simulation-as-creativity (as in Nietzsche/Deleuze), or the expression of value moving through commodities (as in Marx) — although all these ideas are adjacent and useful. But writing as a slicking, smearing or licking across surfaces without depth. Not surface as 'lost-depth', or 'surface' as reduced from a condition of 'polyvalence and complexity' but surface as always-forever-superficial as a slipping of the REAL of appearance (as power). Like the concrete surfaces smeared with vomit in Laura Oldfield-Ford's *Savage Messiah* blog. Like the bloody surface of the face of that woman over there, expressed in the rippling surface of water '… water seeking its liquidity in the sunlight rippling across the cypresses in the back of the garden.'[35] Like the surface of caves — al Qaeda terror compounds in the Tora Bora mountains articulated in the surfaces of US military tactics.[36] Like the carapaces of cockroaches transforming the crucifixion into a swarm tree — 'a fountain crystalled underneath with geometry'.[37] As Dean Kenning writes, a sliding 'away from the fertile corpse of a dismal homogenising individualism, from which anyway-already, sprouts unrecognised phenomena, as the technical transformations of collective rhythms.'[38] As a contestation (or sliding) of/on the 'sense' of things.

A young boy picks his way through the rubble towards their table. People shout at him in the background, gesturing to him to return to the safety cordon in the distance. The area has not been declared safe as yet. Both the structural integrity of the building and the potential of secondary explosive bombs are in question. His face streaked with tears, he stumbles towards them. His face suddenly cracks as he sees a figure on the floor, half covered with rubble. Perhaps he recognises the clothing. He runs forward, brushing off dust and stone and clasps the figure to him crying uncontrollably. Mother? Sister? Impossible to tell. The face is blown off and all that remains is a bloody mass. It is a female figure. Medics pull him off and lead him away as he screams out.

The badger's eyes are bright with excitement: 'This sounds increasingly OK to me. Whereas "literature" summons up comfortable images of stable subjectivity and authorship which align themselves with (static) structures of power as opposed to change, the writer should align themselves technically with transforming, shifting surfaces of production, and the various idiocies and non-idiocies therewith, not to track the progress of capital but to pull back the common property of the collective, of the multiple, of the legion …'

The badger picks up a piece of glass and scratches the following words into a bloody torso nearby — the tip of his tongue poking between his teeth as he concentrates on carving the letters into flesh: 'Performing the emergence of writing itself — in and as its own emergence/articulation — as a writing onto/into the fabric of the articulation of the surface of things — on/in the surfaces of current technique/technology/social-technology, as the rhythm or context where language is (always-already) disengaged from meaning (as the dull narcotic of "Truth"), whether this writing moves like the coilings of the economics and politics of oil production (Negarestani); twists to the rhythm of death and smashed

33 Head Gallery, 'Liam Gillick, An Abrupt Treatise on the Discursive Harmonization of Trade Union Voting Strategies and Conservation Platforms XIII–XVI, 30 November to 29 December'. Available online at http://headgallery.org/current9.html.

34 Benjamin, op. cit., p. 775.

35 Alphonso Lingis, *The Imperative*, Indiana University Press, Bloomington, 1998, p. 29.

36 Reza Negarestani, *Cyclonopedia: Complicity with Anonymous Materials*, Re. Press, Melbourne, 2008, pp. 55–56.

37 Hakim Bey, *T.A.Z. The Temporary Autonomous Zone, Ontological Anarchy, Poetic Terrorism*, available online at http://hermetic.com/bey/taz1.html.

38 Dean Kenning, 'Metallurgy of the Subject', talk delivered at Banner Repeater, London, 30 April 2011.

up bodies (Guyotat); stutters in the coded breakdown of cybernetics (Siratori); drifts as the violence of urban degeneration (Oldfield-Ford), blushes as the colouring of ape's anuses (Bataille); balloons as the tumourous swelling of cancer (Atkins); swirls as the glistening of shifting viscera (McCormack); squawks as ventroliquised dummy-parroting (Holder), as the joy of high school massacre (Howe); as ecstatic internet sales-pitching (Killian); as pedicure agit-prop stylings (Hanns Eisler); as synchopated machine-orgasm (Young-Hae Chang); as karaoke horror-expressionism (Acker); as techno-voodoo (Cussans); as hairdresser dialectics (Freee); or as anonymous porn-abjection (Blowfly-girl), not to forget many others (some already mentioned).[39] Writing on the surface of things, as the cadences and rhythm of articulation / affect / transformation / transduction: for instance, the surface of finger-mind-eye-politics-face-genitals-collective-internet-plants-planes-fairies -bombs-shit-cars-water-death. Because anyway we're all going to be dead soon.'

But then the badger looks in front of him. Again there are not two people there. Just two shattered bodies streaked in blood. The badger turns sadly, sighs and climbs back down the wall.

A nurse in blue uniform comes up to their table. The nurse looks in front of her: two figures, one blown backwards into her chair, face skewed off and another figure slumped forward into his blood on the table. Helen propped back in her chair, white face. Her companion Rodrego slumped forward. A piece of metal lodged in his neck. Blood drips off the table surface onto the floor. One drop at a time, each catching the light for a second. Helen's body — bloody, with clothes half blown off — cranks itself up upon one arm, perversely twisting the torso upwards, against the logic of gravity, into a grotesque one-handed handstand and then blows hundreds of butterflies out of its anus.

39   Reza Negarestani, *Cyclonopedia: Complicity with Anonymous Materials*, Pierre Guyotat, various; Kenji Siratori, *Blood Electric*, Creation Books, London, 2002; Laura Oldfield-Ford, http://lauraoldfieldford.blogspot.com; George Bataille, various; Ed Atkins, *A Tumour (In English)*, 2011; Will Holder's live performance after a Simon Amstell stand-up via earphone, 2012; Rachel Howe, 'Hell on Earth', *Frozen Tears II*, Article Press, Birmingham, 2007; Kevin Killian, *Selected Amazon Reviews*, Hooke Press, 2007; Patricia McCormack, *Cinesexuality*, Ashgate, 2008; Hanns Eisler, *Nail Salon*, http://www.hannseislernailsalon.com; Young-Hae Chang, *Heavy Industries*, http://www.yhchang.com/CUNNILINGUS_IN_NORTH_KOREA.html; Kathy Acker, various; John Cussans, http://codeless88.wordpress.com/; Freee, *The Whistleblower's Pocket Guide to Dissent in the Public Sphere*, Eastside Projects, Birmingham, 2011; Blowfly-girl, http://blowflygirl.blogspot.com/.

Lust

Sam Hasler

Here is lust. Here we go, here we go, here we go, here we go. Gather round. *It's happening again*. I am talking again. Building again, on the quicksand again, crunching those muscles again. I am a transformer, a process and through me flows the code. I keep its droll roll going. I keep the words on the road. I'm kicking them along. Cracking the whip at their heels. Get on with it! Zero one zero zero zero one one zero one …

OK, OK … Here we go. I start a new transmission. With the sun gone low, radio on low. Set the volume now. Sift out your boring thoughts. In to the talk time tonight, wave me on through … Listen to me.

Here is the lust I promised. A new routine. I start tonight's code with nasty little lust. I start here because we are all in here. Don't kid yourself; you're not above. We're going out at night. The radio, the words are structured into night code. Lust is surely a night code. Lust is a nocturnal boy in his nocturnal loneliness. Lust says 'It is only a stupid joke'. You should be feeling a bit of silliness. You should be feeling a tiny twitch, a tongue of titillation, one heart-beat chasing down the next. Cheap lurches into the guts. Here he is. Lusty and damned. All bad. A screwy foe. A slippery slope … Down and down … slippery and screwy … and down …

Molten rock bottom. Hot bottom. Hot bottom on the radar. Rolling on walking legs … If you think this is low, wait till we get there.

Bottom. Bottom rolling on lucid legs. Safe and resistant. Lucky leg jelly. Just a slight lifted line of underwear. Shapely light lifted lines. Bouncy bottom bun. Lifting and dropping in the turn, over the lucky legs.

The mind drives in, surpassing any physical realm with imaginary ease. Under the fabric, under the underwear into a whole darkness. In the dewy darkness trying to calm down. Damn up those rivers. Cruddy hell, Calm down! Twitcher. An inadvertent sniff of the air. There, holy well! A deep pool. The undercover scent of slightly overripe soft fruit. Sugary. Then the ping-pong of bread crust, salt and bitter herbs. Are those your pants Bambi?

With a giant hoik! Those gazonuous gazungas! Holy blow. What a crime that such trol-loping mammaries can trot so fun-a-go-round and never be rolled under my clamy paws. Then what dark mistrust, not cruel but cutting. Dismissive. Skin like evening sand. Moonless midnight lolls over the shoulder and writes a childlike line across her forehead. She surfs her hair and body with skill. Surfer baby. Yeah baby!

Oh my dumb gob's so full of sticky toffee and senseless stupidity.

But back to that black hair that is blue with the light. A force field helmet of energy tendrils. Sexy sadness in the picture face. It's a sci-fi kind of sadness. Staring out into the field of stars as far as too far away. Eyes are pathetic tools against the whole of space. She can't talk to me! Her and the cruddy space world. My awful world. My dumb gob.

Commissioned for exhibitions and performance readings, Motto, 13.5.11; White Columns, 22.10.11 to 19.11.11; Space, 6.4.12 to 20.5.12.

Fuck '68, I'd rather '69!

Stewart Home

The idea of the archive has proved fashionable in discourse about visual culture over the past decade,[1] and made those — including me — who have engaged with marginal post-Fluxus practices such as mail art (which placed a premium on personal archives) appear alluring in relation to this.[2] The archive of my mail art and underground publishing activities was acquired by the National Art Library at the Victoria & Albert Museum, London in 1999. More recently a retrospective of my work has been shown at both White Columns, New York, and SPACE, London, as a part of Book Works' ongoing *Again, A Time Machine*, 2011–12, project based around archives. My mini retrospective was, of course, archival in nature and drew on both visual works and publications.

Another example of an artist with an interest in the archive is Pete Horobin, who created an extraordinary record of his own life during the 1980s as he worked out of a space he dubbed the DATA Attic in Dundee. Born in London in the final month of 1949, Horobin moved to Fife in Scotland when he was twelve-years-old, and attended Duncan of Jordanstone College of Art in Dundee in the early '70s. After graduating, Horobin became fascinated by the creative process and in an attempt to break it down and understand it, began to record many aspects of his existence. Starting on the first day of 1980, Horobin initiated his *DATA Project* (Daily Action Time Archive). *DATA* was pre-planned as a decade-long event that would document Horobin's life from the ages of thirty to forty. This included a daily 'DATA sheet' to record each day of the 1980s, films, cassettes, videos, photography, paintings, the clothes Horobin wore, once they were worn out and even the packaging of the consumer goods he

1 This interest in the archive is also evident in events such as the day conference *Consensus Contention: Performing The Archive* at the University of Ulster during 22–23 June 2007. Staying in Ulster, Adam Broomberg and Oliver Chanarin worked with the archives of the Belfast Exposed photography workshops to explore how the material stored at this site has been read and reread. Broomberg and Chanarin went on to discuss the work that emerged from their research in Ulster — and in other historical collections around the world — as part of the conference *Out of the Archive: Artists, Images and History*, Tate Modern, London, November 2011.

2 I deal with Pete Horobin — who was active in the mail art network throughout the 1980s — in this essay; but I also have in mind other mail art figures such as Ulises Carrión who was the subject of a posthumous partial retrospective at The Showroom in London entitled *Gossip, Scandal and Good Manners*, 2–26 June 2010.

used (soap boxes and food cartons etc.). Added to this were art works Horobin exchanged with others both within and outside the international mail art network. For much of the 1980s Horobin claimed unemployment benefits, and so this archive simultaneously served to record aspects of the life of the urban poor in northern Europe during that decade.

I will return to Horobin's extraordinary archive and its fate and then move on to other matters, but first I want to position it in relation to a more general consideration of historical material. An archive is usually deemed to be a unique collection of records rather than data that is replicated elsewhere. However, with the ongoing proliferation and expansion of the Internet this understanding appears to be something that is in the process of mutating.[3] When I first became interested enough in Fluxus and the Situationists in the 1980s to begin researching them, I found myself using archives such as the British Library and the Tate Library at Millbank in London. Since then levels of interest in the subject matter I was exploring three decades ago has increased exponentially, and I can now find online much of what I had to go to libraries and archives for access to in the 1980s.

There was an explosion of interest in the Situationists from 1989 onwards, and a slower but equally spectacular rise in the amount of published material about Fluxus from a few years before that. Mention of the Situationists was largely absent from twentieth-anniversary celebrations of the uprisings of May '68 in 1988, but the group became a far greater presence in fortieth-anniversary festivities commemorating the same events.[4] Of course perceptions of the actual role the Situationists played in the occupations movement in France will always be to some degree subjective — and the way it has waxed rather than waned in the past twenty years is a good illustration of this. Talking to intelligent twenty-something students doing research into the Situationists today, it can be difficult to get them to understand that few people were interested in this group until the end of the 1980s. Most students who are young enough not to remember a time when there was little interest in the Situationists, find it hard to square recent academic eulogies of Debord and his cohorts against the fact that for twenty years after May '68 they were not perceived by most writers on the subject as historically important actors within it.[5]

A point to remember here is that archives may be a form of raw data for historical researchers but their interpretation is always to a degree subjective.[6] This is not to say anything goes as history — since many assertions are historically disprovable — it is merely to underline that neither is it completely objective.[7] Emphasis within and interpretation of historical materials always entails a subjective element. That said, historical interpretations predicated on — for example — the 'great man theory' that has its origins in the overblown romanticism of Thomas Carlyle, and which totally ignore complex social factors in favour of biographies of 'heroes', are so simplistic that those with a serious interest in human sciences are unlikely to take them seriously. So while facts can be shown to be erroneous, certain methodological approaches are also so obviously flawed that they can be discounted as well.

Returning to Pete Horobin's *DATA Project*, its all-encompassing and expansive nature resulted in it being a difficult art work to offload once it was completed. Not only did it contain the residues of one man's daily and creative life for a whole decade, it also documented

3   To give an indication of how online archives change our relationship to the information they contain, I'll provide a personal example. For nearly a decade I've been championing Terry Taylor's reforgotten drug novel *Baron's Court, All Change*, London, MacGibbon & Kee, 1961, and was very excited when it was finally republished in November 2011. Searching online for coverage of the reissue, I came across an original 1961 review from the *Tribune* newspaper. It was short but positive, and simultaneously served to remind me that for years I'd been meaning to search for the book reviews Taylor told me he'd written for *Tribune*. This task wasn't a priority but since it appeared I could now do it easily online rather than trudging through old newspapers at the British Library, I immediately searched for Taylor by name in the *Tribune* online archive. I found three reviews apparently credited to him. I was surprised by their dating since from what Taylor had told me, it seemed he'd written for the paper a few years before these pieces appeared. They were also very roughly scanned with one apparently having been mistakenly read across columns, thereby rendering it nonsensical.

I sent Taylor links to the pieces and asked him about them. I assumed they must have been heavily (and also rather poorly) edited because the prose didn't read like anything I'd seen by Terry. The reply Taylor emailed me on Thursday, 8 December, 2011 only made the matter more puzzling. 'Thanks so much for your email and what could have been quotes from stuff I wrote for *Tribune*. I find most of it a mystery. I'm 93% certain that I didn't write this stuff. Although I wish I'd written one of them as Bill Burroughs himself couldn't have put together a slicker cutup. But no. This stuff wasn't from my hand. But yet again something is whispering from the back of my old thinking box that I did review a book by someone called Laurie. Another thing is I don't think I wrote for them in 1964 / 1965. It would have been earlier, much nearer the publication of *BCAC*. I do remember that the literary editor was called Elizabeth something-or-other at the time I wrote for them, so perhaps that's an important clue. Colin MacInnes introduced me to her. I was paid very little but when visiting her office she gave me piles of review copies which I used to flog in a Charing X Rd bookshop.'

Taylor's name appears to be on the original pieces and the subject matter of the three reviews are in his subject area — drugs and youth culture. That said, after getting Taylor's email I wondered whether there was someone with the same name and interests as him writing for *Tribune* in the 1960s; or possibly an editor who didn't want their name appearing on reviews dealing with drugs and so they borrowed Taylor's moniker, simply because it was convenient for them to do so. Having looked for various names and book titles in the *Tribune* online archive, I found its search engine wasn't particularly reliable at finding the information I sought, and it is quite possible that there are other Terry Taylor reviews (hopefully by the writer who interests me) that I haven't yet found. You can check out the *Tribune* online archive here: http://archive.tribunemagazine.co.uk/about.

4   Likewise, as a visitor to *Fluxus and the Essential Questions of Life*, Grey Art Gallery, New York, September – December 2011, I was amused by the show of related works in the basement beneath the main gallery that 'contextualised' it. Among other things this background exhibition included documentation of 1960s happenings. When Mark Bloch (who I went to these shows with) and I were first becoming engaged with contemporary art in the 1970s, the hap-

penings movement was much better known than Fluxus — now this situation has been reversed. To us this was a matter for quiet laughter when we attended the shows together in November 2011. Younger people visiting the exhibitions would have a very different relationship to — and knowledge of — the material on show.

5   See *French Revolution: 1968* by Patrick Seale and Maureen McConville, Heinemann / Penguin, London, 1968, for one example of the many pre-1989 works that don't give the Situationists much — if any — space, or credit them with any importance in relation to the May events. Likewise, critical thinking about the Situationists is in part so badly deformed because much of the writing in this subject area is academic. Peer review of academic papers mitigates against critical appraisal of the subjects under discussion. Academics are so dependent for career advancement upon other specialists within their area that most are afraid to shake things up and organise material into new paradigms or view it from new perspectives — no matter how erroneous the consensus academic view on any particular subject may be. Similarly, the didactic and hierarchical nature of university teaching clearly discourages critical thinking among students. Acting as if they are somehow stuck in the nineteenth century, most university professors attempt to position themselves as experts handing down truths from on high. Year in and year out such attitudes serve to ensure there is an intellectually inert and docile crop of graduates and post-graduates. This contrasts sharply with the learning environment provided by online sites such as Wikipedia — which, despite their many faults are not reliant on the kind of conformism essential to academic success.

6   It is also important to remember that just because something is recorded in an archive — no matter how official — it does not follow that it is factually correct. Researching my own family history, I discovered that my paternal grandfather had different places and dates of birth recorded on his birth and death certificates. It logically follows that one of them must be wrong — and it is of course more likely that the record closest to the event is correct (although likelihood is not proof).

7   It is possible to give many examples of claims that are historically disprovable but I'll stick with one firm favourite, the assertions Howard Marks has made about Graham Plinston's dope bust — the event which provided Marks with his break into big time drug dealing. Since I've dealt with this before I'll simply quote from a footnote to my essay 'Voices Green & Purple' included in *Summer of Love: Psychedelic Art, Social Crisis and Counterculture in the 1960s* edited by Christoph Grunenberg and Jonathan Harris, Liverpool University Press and Tate Liverpool, Liverpool, 2005.

'… while invoking Graham Plinston's 1970 bust in Lorrach as a key event in the Howard Marks story, both David Leigh in his authorised biography *High Time: The Life & Times of Howard Marks*, Unwin, London, 1985, and Howard Marks in his autobiography *Mr Nice*, Vintage, London, 1998 omit to mention that rather than being alone, Plinston was arrested and subsequently jailed alongside Geoff Thompson.

In his autobiography, Howard Marks is two months out in his dating of the Lorrach bust. The fact that Marks and those drawing on his recollections get their facts wrong can be demonstrated easily enough by consulting press reports of the time. A Reuters news agency wire of 18 March 1970 led, for example, to coverage on page 5 of the London Times the following day headlined "Britons

the underground art networks of which he was a part. The *DATA Project* required a considerable amount of storage space, and it would be expensive to catalogue in terms of the work hours required to do so. Horobin spent many years trying to find an institution that would either buy or accept his *DATA Project* as a gift — in part because once he found a home for it he would no longer need to keep on the Dundee flat in which it was housed. Nearly two decades after Horobin's *DATA Project* was completed, Artpool in Budapest agreed they'd take much — but not all — of the archive. Artpool was founded in 1979 by György Galántai and Júlia Klaniczay. It functioned as a hub for the type of avant-garde activity disliked by those in charge of Hungary's official culture prior to the collapse of the Eastern Bloc. It went on to become an archive of international activity in mail art and other ephemeral aesthetic forms with their roots in Fluxus and related movements.

What interested Artpool in the archive of the *DATA Project* was Horobin's collection of mail art. Much of the other material he'd collected as part of his project was either destroyed or passed on to other people. Not just letters I'd written to Horobin — but also many publications (produced by both me and others) I'd given or sent to him — were returned to me because Artpool had limited resources and little interest in these materials. I collected much of what was returned to me from Horobin's flat, and while I was there, saw him destroy and bin a number of his own artworks. I see this editing process as reducing the historic value of the archive, but the effect on its aesthetic worth is more debatable.[8] That said, archives are often broken up and destroyed, and this, as well as the very process of their formation has an effect on what comes to be written as history. There is also a chance element in the way people encounter archives. I came into contact with Pete Horobin in April 1984 after seeing a listing in *Performance* magazine for an upcoming Neoist Apartment Festival he was organising in London. Had this event been held in Birmingham or Dundee rather than London, it is unlikely I would have got to know him or become intimately familiar with his archive.

Moving on and focusing on a very different archive will further illustrate just how hit and miss it is for people to come across material that has been gathered together on a voluntary basis. When my book *The Assault On Culture* was published in Lithuania, I went to stay with my translator Redas Derzys in Alytus. There aren't many tourist attractions in southern Lithuania and so I visited most of those in or close to my translator's hometown. I was puzzled and intrigued by a listing I saw on an A4 tourist information sheet for the local Afghan War Veterans Museum. Only a telephone number was given (no address). I asked my host about it and he said he had never heard of the museum. Redas called the number and arranged a visit to the archive. We were given a time to go to an address in a residential section of Alytus — and Redas came along to translate for me, because no one at the museum spoke English. Had I not been with my Lithuanian translator who was able to interpret for me, I would not have been able to arrange the visit. Before we arrived, local veterans assembled a display of material they thought would interest us.

It transpired the museum had started in the 1980s as a drinking club for local Afghan War veterans. After the club was officially registered with the authorities in 2003, these get-togethers evolved into various projects, including the museum, which came into being towards the end of 2006 (about eighteen months before my first visit — and with much help from the Mayor of Alytus, who secured the premises in which it is housed). Still doubling as a social and drinking club, the museum takes the form of an archive of memorabilia collected by the veterans and occupies a ground floor apartment in a social housing block. The museum's holdings consist mainly of snapshot photographs and 'memory albums', visual diaries compiled by individual soldiers during their tours of duty in Afghanistan. These materials are curated both by and from the perspective of ordinary soldiers who had no wish to serve Soviet imperialism, but were forced to do so. During our translated conversation they were less forthcoming in expressing any negative views on United States led NATO imperialism, but when I persisted with the topic and they realised my views, they did say that the local population in Afghanistan would see no difference between US and Soviet forces.

During the Soviet occupation of Afghanistan, 1979–89, some 5,000 Lithuanians were conscripted into the army and sent there, in many cases (and certainly in the cases of all the members of the Alytus Afghan War Veterans Club) against their will. Lithuanian conscripts and those from neighbouring Baltic States were serving an imperial power. In order to quell potential dissent among Baltic soldiers, efforts were made to separate them into different regiments — which meant there were limited opportunities for them to speak their own languages or to engage with members of their own communities (the language of the Soviet army was Russian and the use of Baltic tongues was very actively discouraged). The average age of these men when they began military service was nineteen. The occupation of Afghanistan claimed numerous lives, and also caused immense material and psychological damage before finally ending in defeat for the USSR.

In 1990, when Lithuania regained its independence following the collapse of the Soviet Union, the Afghan war was treated as a major political mistake and its veterans were seen as part of the Soviet legacy, beyond the concern of Lithuanian politicians and public who neither celebrated them as heroes, nor recognised them as victims. Injured soldiers received no compensation from the new Lithuanian state, and were unable to claim allowances from the

Held On Drugs Charge". This report makes it clear that both Plinston and Geoff Thompson were in jail after the discovery of "about 105lbs of hashish in their car", and that they had been arrested upon entering Germany "from Switzerland on February 26". The Times piece explicitly cites information contained within it as being provided by a British consulate spokesman in Stuttgart, and the authorities notified Thompson and Plinston's families of the arrests before speaking to the press about them.'

Therefore it is ridiculous of David Leigh to assert in his authorised Howard Marks biography *High Time* that in the spring of 1970 Mandy Plinston sent Marks to Frankfurt to investigate her dope smuggling partner's disappearance. As should already be clear, Mandy Plinston knew of the bust before Howard Marks; as did my mother Julia Callan-Thompson, my mother's boyfriend of the time Bruno de Galzain, Geoff Thompson's partner of the time Jane Ripley, Charlie Radcliffe, Alex Trocchi and many others immersed in the London counterculture. The claim made by Leigh and some later writers to the

effect that Howard Marks learnt of the bust by looking through German newspapers in Frankfurt, and then relayed this "discovery" back to the UK, is utterly spurious. Its reiteration demonstrates the rather dubious status of a number of texts that claim to provide inside information on the dope trade.'

8   Despite its partial destruction it is still possible to use the DATA archive to kick start debates around issues like whether arts funding or blanket welfare provision is the best way of inducing aesthetic excellence among artists. For much of the eighties, Pete Horobin who created the DATA Project claimed unemployment benefits and was markedly unsuccessful at attaining arts grants. In some ways the selective manner in which Artpool have cherry picked what they are preserving from this archive serves to heighten our awareness of this particular issue — because arts grants are also handed out in a selective manner (in stark contrast to the universal welfare benefits available in the UK in the 1980s).

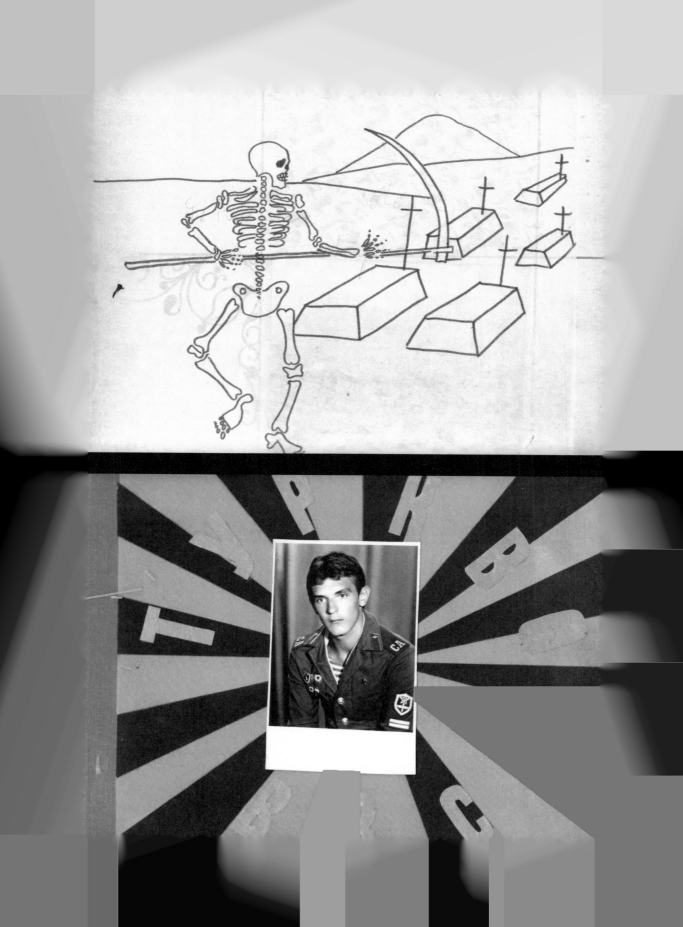

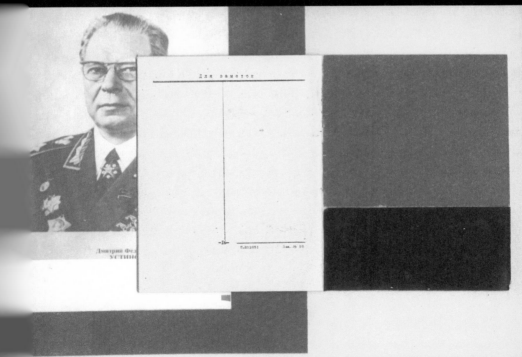

Дмитрий Фед...
УСТИНО...

-16-

Г-212651   Зак. № 10

defunct USSR. The only official acknowledgement that Lithuanian Afghan War veterans were in any way victims of the Soviet system was made in 2007, when they were issued with certificates to replace Soviet ones which had become invalid in 1990 (but these did not entitle them to compensation). The period during which Lithuania and its neighbours were a part of the Soviet Union is now popularly viewed by Baltic citizens as one of occupation — and there is little sympathy among much of the population for those who were conscripted into the Soviet army.

Among the most interesting items in the Afghan War Veterans Museum were the soldiers' personal scrapbooks. The albums are hand made and mostly contain a mixture of photographs and cartoons. Both scrapbooks and photographs were officially forbidden — to prevent intelligence about the Afghan War inadvertently falling into the wrong hands — but I understand virtually all the soldiers involved in the conflict made them. Some higher ranking officers turned a blind eye to the albums and in a few instances provided material for them, whereas other officers confiscated them — and in some cases punished those caught making them.

One of the key functions of a traditional museum is to preserve objects for the future. Nonetheless, even on my first visit to the Alytus Afghan War Veterans Museum in 2008, many of the albums and photographs I viewed were beginning to deteriorate. Those running the museum didn't appear particularly bothered by this, since what they were doing was first and foremost for themselves — and the idea that their collection should be preserved after their deaths didn't seem to make much sense to them. The scrapbooks I viewed were to me incredible examples of folk art, and I wanted more people to see them. So did my translator Redas Derzys, since he was both a practising artist and the head of the local art school. When I returned to Alytus in August 2009 for the local biennial organised by Derzys, we were able to take the various international artists in attendance on a trip to the Afghan War Veterans Museum. This was the year in which the flow of visitors to the museum — about 500 in 2009 — reached its peak.

I made another trip to Alytus in 2011 for the most recent biennial, and once again we both encouraged international participants to make a trip to the Veterans Museum. Among those who did so was Ben Morea, a man who had long fascinated me. I'd spent much of the 1980s tracking down the material produced by the radical Black Mask and Motherfucker groups in which Morea had played a key role in the 1960s. I had even travelled to New York in March 1989 to search for various publications issued by this group, but drew a blank there. Eventually I found most of what I was looking for in private collections in the UK, and the documents I collected together were finally published as *Black Mask and Up Against The Wall Motherfucker* in 1993.[9] Talking with Morea in Lithuania and more recently in New York, gave me further insight into his three decades as a leading light among the disappeared — since for nearly thirty years virtually no one knew where to find him. Morea told me that by 1969 he felt things were getting too hot for him and so he vanished into New Mexico, where he camped out in the mountains for five years. He informed me this was followed by a more settled life — but one lived mainly among the Native American community rather than the political and artistic milieus from which he'd risen to notoriety.

Morea was, and still is, deeply involved in Peyote ceremonies. He told me he only reappeared on the activist scene because the political and ecological state of the world was so desperate that he felt he had to do something about it. Partly due to my efforts with the publication and subsequent reprint of *Black Mask and Up Against the Wall Motherfucker*, and Morea's own reappearance on the scene in New York, at both activist meetings on campuses and at Occupy Wall Street, Morea's activities between 1966 and 1969 are becoming better known. To give a few examples, the Black Mask group dumped uncollected rubbish from the Lower East Side into a fountain outside the Lincoln Center on 12 February 1968 (during a NYC refuse collection strike). This event was publicised in advance with a leaflet entitled *We Propose A Culture Exchange (Garbage For Garbage)*. Another stunt from the Black Mask period, which ended in May 1968 (when Morea took to the streets with his Motherfuckers collective), was shooting the poet Kenneth Koch using a real gun loaded with blank bullets (apparently the writer fainted). With equal aplomb, Black Mask disrupted a public art lecture by making up flyers giving the date, time and location of the event and handing these out to the homeless — who turned up in some numbers to claim the free drink that had been intended for the bourgeoisie. I reused the ruse in London in the 1990s to disrupt the smooth running of the spectacle surrounding the Booker Prize (or rather the dinner before it is announced). As my Booker prank illustrates, the archive can be used playfully as well as historically. I've been able to bring quite a number of anti-art stunts back into use, documentation of which was included in the archival show at White Columns and at SPACE, as well as in some of my books, including *Confusion Incorporated: A Collection of Lies, Hoaxes and Hidden Truths*.[10]

I found Morea charismatic and his life story absolutely incredible. He told me he'd left home at seventeen and shacked up with The Living Theatre, while attending John Cage composition classes at The New School. From around 1963 onwards, Morea was involved with Group Center and participated in their astonishing happenings, as well as developing as a painter under the influence of Aldo Tambellini (the beating heart of the Group Center collective). Back in the 1980s I knew nothing of this, and so Black Mask and the Motherfuckers were for me both a mystery and a challenge. Much of their material was unavailable, but the little that I'd seen made researching them seem much more enticing than looking at the 1968 occupations movement in France (which I thought was already well documented — and in many ways the work on it then was preferable to what is being done now, with the more recent and I feel historically untenable bigging up of the Situationist International).

Throughout the 1980s and 1990s I heard many tales about what had happened to Ben Morea after he dropped from public view. Some people claimed that he was dead, others that he'd become a millionaire car dealer in Arizona and had rejected radical politics in favour of a pro-capitalist stance. None of the stories I heard were true but the aura of obscurity surrounding Morea and the Motherfuckers led me to use the slogan 'fuck '68, I'd rather '69' when speaking to friends about the occupations movement during its various anniversaries.

9   Edited by Stewart Home as Jacques Vaché, *Black Mask and Up Against the Wall Motherfucker, the Incomplete Works of Ron Hahne, Ben Morea and the Black Mask Group*, Unpopular Books, and Sabotage Editions, London, 1993.

10 Stewart Home, *Confusion Incorporated: A Collection of Lies, Hoaxes and Hidden Truths*, Codex, Hove, 1999.

That said, having met and spent time with Ben Morea, I'm happy to leave filling in the history of Black Mask and The Motherfuckers to others. I feel I know enough and I want to move on … If I spoke Russian or Lithuanian I might well be tempted to do some work around the art and archives of the Alytus Afghan War Veterans. Since I lack these language skills, my focus is elsewhere. The lost history of the European counterculture as revealed through the life of my mother has been one of the things that's occupied me for the past decade.[11] I guess I'm always searching for something yet more abstruse, because I prefer new horizons to well-trodden ground … This is partly a matter of temperament, but anyone with a healthy curiosity ought to prefer discovering something new and overturning old paradigms to going through familiar material one more time! Those who continue to turn over received history uncritically — with one eye on academic advancement and the other on their own navels — are not just digging their own graves, they're zombies who are already dead!

11   I not only based my novel *Tainted Love*, Virgin, London, 2005 on my research into my mother's life, but have also produced a great deal of both non-fiction and visual material drawing on the same investigations. Terry Taylor — mentioned in footnote 1 above — is merely one example of a writer I came across through this research. He was a friend of my mother in the 1960s and 1970s.

Demo Penfold Street: an artist's presentation
Claire Makhlouf Carter

In advance of the presentation:

• Artist to participate in a one-night event situated in a gallery or seminar room with moveable furniture. Artist to secure a parking space nearby for the duration of the event.

• Artist to contact the following people on the understanding they will contribute to an artist's presentation concerned with self-immolation and smell.

• To employ one female presenter; one passive indicator sniffer dog and handler. To organise three volunteers.

• Artist to provide the volunteers with the full script and a schedule (end of script) and to inform the volunteers they will receive £20.00 expenses.

• Artist to instruct the presenter, dog handler and volunteers to be available for the duration of the event and keep their instructions and roles secret.

• Artist to instruct the volunteers to bring a bag and a spare sock to the event; the dog handler to train the dog to find semtex on a person rather than on a static object and be prepared to recite three lines of dialogue; the presenter to memorise four short sections of the text.

• Artist to purchase six 250ml UN certified white wide-neck canisters with tamper evident lids; six packets of gauze pads; six polythene envelopes large enough to contain the canisters; one black metal 20-litre petrol jerrycan; box of long matches; one pen; three 180ml airtight containers; three pairs of latex gloves; three 50ml bottles of antiseptic hand gel; 100ml spray bottle containing SerenaScent perfume; one deodorant stick; one lighter; one change of clothes.

• Artist to source one over-sized handbag; one mic; amp and speakers; thirty stackable chairs; one small table; one large table; three semtex papers.

• Artist to print twelve contracts (see prototype end of script). A brown envelope containing one twenty-pound note to be attached with a paperclip to six of the contracts.

• Artist to remove the email (pages 193–94) from the presenter's script and fold in four. To place folded email and script in the over-sized handbag.

• Artist to place one semtex paper in each 180ml airtight container.

• Artist to address and stamp the polythene envelopes to DARPA: Defense Advanced Research Projects Agency, 3701 North Fairfax Drive, Arlington, Virginia 22203-1714.

The day of the presentation:

• Artist surreptitiously to: pass over-sized handbag to the presenter; pass each volunteer a pair of latex gloves, one bottle of antiseptic hand gel and one airtight container containing semtex paper. Volunteers to store items in their bags.

• Artist to imagine the room divided into three sections -- to designate the first section as a stage, the second section as an auditorium in which to seat the visitors, the third section as an off-stage area in which to situate the bar.

• In the stage area artist to move one chair; one small table; one mic; one petrol jerrycan; one box of long matches; six packets of gauze papers; six 250ml canisters (with lids off); twelve contracts -- six with money attached; one pen; six plastic envelopes; one SerenaScent spray bottle.

• In the stage area artist to position the chair left of centre and facing towards the auditorium. To move the small table in front of the chair.

• Artist to set up the mic in front of the table angled towards the chair; the amp and speakers to demarcate the front corners of the stage area.

• Artist to place the petrol jerrycan adjacent to the amp with the box of long matches resting on the can's handles.

• Artist to balance on the top surface of one speaker the 250ml canisters and lids; the packets of gauze pads; the plastic envelopes; the pile of contracts; the pen and the SerenaScent spray bottle. (To be balanced ad hoc).

• In the auditorium artist to arrange the stacking chairs to face the stage.

• In the off-stage area artist to move the large table to be used as a bar.

Presenter's script:

Presenter and artist are both sitting with the audience. The presenter sits in the third row from the front. The artist sits two rows behind. At the designated time the presenter (Rachel) walks in from the audience with the over-sized bag and sits at the table. She removes the presenter's script from the bag and picks up the first sheet of paper. Over this the artist (Claire) switches her seat to where Rachel was sitting.

RACHEL

Somber and serious, flat tone -- understated.

> Wednesday, 14 August 2010, Herat Regional Hospital, Afghanistan: Anoosheh (whose name has been changed because of her age) lies in a hospital bed with third-degree burns covering 38% of her body and ash coating the inside of her lungs. Her physician, Dr. Abdul Raheem Khidr, believes it's unlikely she will survive.
>
> In the next bed is 14-year-old Fareiba (her name has also been changed). Her neck and torso look as if they have been turned inside out: the flesh is a raw, wet, oozing pink. She grimaces as she talks. 'I was tired of life,' she says, her voice flat. Fareiba was 11 when she was married. Unlike Anoosheha, her tormentor was a woman -- a senior wife of her brother in law. 'Sometimes she would beat me and pull my hair out and prevent me from taking water from the pump,' Fareiba says. It appears as if Fareiba and her sister in law were competing over food and resources.
>
> The household was poor, made up of four families struggling in the same living space. Dr. Abdul Raheem Khidr cites not abusive family conditions but a more commonly accepted explanation. 'Most of these patients have emotional, psychological problems,' he says standing over the girls' bed.

Rachel pauses, and looks up. This section to be memorised.

RACHEL

Unfortunately Claire Makhlouf Carter cannot be with us today
and I have been asked to present her work.

Claire is busy with a show in Tunisia, the subject being self-
immolation.

Rachel picks up a new piece of paper.

RACHEL

During the holiday break I read a play by Peter Brooke called
'us or US' Inserted at the back of the text is a photograph taken in South Vietnam by Malcolm Browne. It is of the
Buddhist monk Thích Quảng Đức; 釋廣德;(tich kwong duuk) set-
ting himself alight. Witnesses say the monk did not move or
make a sound. The background depicts people walking past as if
nothing unusual is happening. Despite thorough investigation
I could not find any contemporaneous accounts describing the
smell of burning flesh.

Rachel picks up new piece of paper.

RACHEL

Claire adds: The photograph of the monk is a Translucent
Screen Saver veiling her vision of the world. The monk's presence resides at the back of her eyes. In 2001 this condition
was medically recognised as TSS Syndrome. Currently there are
more than 6,000 reported cases of TSS in the UK. Research suggests up to 60% of individuals who experience panic attacks
may develop TSS. A particular TSS can last for months, sometimes years. It is almost impossible to obliterate a TSS
although it can be substituted with a new one.

Occasionally Claire is so desperate to substitute her TSS
she invents new experiences in the hope they will trigger a
replacement. For example while researching self-immolation
Claire attempted to override the TSS by concentrating on the
subject of body odour. She researched the Kreimer vs. Tate
Gallery case in which the Court of Appeal upheld a gallery
rule that stated, 'Visitors whose bodily hygiene is offen-
sive so as to constitute a nuisance to other persons shall be
required to leave the building'. She continued this line of
enquiry by tracking down a Jo Kreimer from South London who

finally agreed to a meeting in the V&A museum. This developed
into daily meetings of approximately one hour for 15 days.
During the meetings Claire breathed deeply to capture Jo's
odour and engaged in as much eye contact as possible. However
this replacement strategy did not work and the burning monk
TSS continues to pervade her vision.

Claire has found she can switch present screen savers to older
ones but only momentarily and the process causes a migraine
attack.

The preceding TSS was of a large dead rabbit lying on her living room carpet. By tracing the smeary contents spilled from
its ruptured intestines she was able to track the rabbit back
to the cat flap. Despite intensive cleaning, the stench from
the ruptured intestines lingered in her house for three weeks.
When Claire switches her TSS momentarily to the rabbit, the
stench recurs. It is a deep dark green earthy scent followed
by a sharp rancid taste in the roof of her mouth.

Claire was pleased her cat presented the dead rabbit as it
replaced her previous TSS, which was of a deceased neighbour. A
phone call from a concerned relative convinced Claire to break
into the neighbour's house. In the kitchen she discovered a man
lying on the concrete floor. The side of his head lay in a blood
puddle. His inflamed tongue and the extreme angle in which it
hung from his open mouth recorded the trauma of his fall.

The dead neighbour TSS consists of a close up of the mouth
region with sharp focus on the flopped out tongue but sometimes shifts back and forth to another close-up of the event
-- an upturned palm splintered with chest hairs. Claire states
the chest hairs became embedded under the skin of her left
hand after her failed attempt at cardiac resuscitation. This
particular TSS comes with the sound of distant shouting. A
woman's telephone voice intermittently urges 'Count louder.
I can't hear you count, press harder'. While picking out the
transplanted hairs with tweezers Claire concluded because the
hairs had stuck to her skin rather than his, she had broken
the bones of a dead person.

Claire has been attempting to record the smell of death.
Burning bodies, ruptured intestines and the odour of the dead
pervading the house.

The first TSS Claire can recall is a small wooden cage with
flames engulfing a Bantam chick. This TSS is accompanied with
the smell and feel of brittle burnt feathers.

For her Tunisian show Claire has instructed the curator to set
up the gallery to resemble a theatre with five rows of chairs
facing an empty space. Placed on each chair a box of matches.
In the empty space there will be a filled petrol can. She wants
to discover the audience response when she douses herself with
the solution. Whether anyone will strike a match. She wants to
test if anyone will attempt to self-immolate during the time
she is not present. She has been negotiating with the health
and safety officer.

For Claire the first TSS of the burning chick was triggered by
an event of love rather than murder. The backdrop is a small-
holding in a remote rural area. It is 1975. To save the chick
from being pecked to death by other chicks Claire persuaded
her father to construct a small cage and her mother to allow
the cage and chick indoors. Knowing the chick needed warmth
she filled a metal brooder with paraffin, lit it and carefully placed the brooder, straw and chick inside the cage. She
recalls rushing into an adjacent room to watch Dr. Who.

Tonight Claire does not want to detect the smell of death, but
the fear of life. She believes the live moment, cannot be felt
by a performer unless they are part of the audience. She wants
to present and watch the presentation simultaneously.

Rachel looks up, searches and stares at Claire who is sitting with
the visitors. This section to be memorised. Rachel focuses mainly on
Claire.

                          RACHEL

This is the second reason Claire provided for employing a presenter. She informed me yesterday the Tunisia show has been
delayed by a week while permissions are sought. I suspect she
has a fear of presenting rather than a fear of life or death.

Rachel pauses.

                          RACHEL

Let me read this email from her.

Rachel pulls out the folded email from the over-sized bag. Claire
stares back at her antagonistically.

From: Claire Carter
Date: 8 February 2012, 18:18
Subject: Demo Penfold Street
To: Rachel Cockburn

Hi Rachel

Thanks for agreeing to present my work.

It is a great comfort to find someone who actually enjoys presenting. As you know because of the panic of presenting the live moment means I sweat profusely, my hands go numb, I experience nausea, chest pain and a smothering sensation. Even if I was paid a fee of £1,000 I would still refuse to subject myself to this type of exposure.

I forgot to mention something in our last meeting. As you know I'm interested in the impossibility of documenting smell. While researching the smell of death which began by concentrating on the act of burning oneself alive ... I became distracted and found some additional information to do with empathy and fear that I think you should be aware of.

I know you are in need of cash so thought this might help. Research funded by the US Defence Advanced Research Projects Agency (DARPA is the Pentagon's military research wing) has discovered when sniffing 'panic sweat', regions of the brain that handle emotional and social signals become far more active. Fear and anxiety trigger the release of a chemical that makes people empathise. This may sound like a positive counter-reaction to fear, but actually results in a realisation that the smell of fear is contagious. The research is of interest to the US military. Isolating the fear pheromone could be utilised in warfare perhaps to induce terror in enemy troops.

Did you know dogs can be trained to sniff out empathy and fear? DAFRA is paying good money for fear pheromone collections. The fee depends on the amount of pheromones collected from sweat glands. This must be collected from a person in a situation that triggers fear in the participant.

Rachel, as repayment for stepping in for me I am organising a sniffer dog and handler to appear in the performance. The handler's name is Tim and the dog's name is Scooby. Tim has trained the dog to find a person in the room who is

proliferating strong fear pheromones. All you have to do is
persuade the visitor to wipe their underarms, palms of hands
and, ideally, the back of knees with gauze pad and place it in
an airtight jar. You could choose to split the money you make
with the visitor; I will leave that up to you. Either way I
think you will make a packet and I know you have an extreme
fear of dogs so I guess the dog may choose you. I know someone
who made $556. He was afraid of flying.

    Best,
    Claire

Rachel puts the email on the table and looks up. This section to be
memorised.

                    RACHEL

    I don't think the dog will pick me out because some of you
    look quite terrified, especially you Claire.

Rachel stares at Claire antagonistically.

                    RACHEL

    I have been asked to inform you that a dog and handler will
    be visiting this room shortly, so if anyone is afraid of
    dogs I suggest this is a good time to leave, although it is
    only fair to let you know that to dissuade visitors leaving
    Claire has suggested I spray the room with this perfume called
    SerenaScent made from the chemicals found in fresh grass cut-
    tings.

Rachel stands holding the next piece of paper and picks up the spray
bottle containing the SerenaScent perfume. Rachel walks into the audi-
torium/off-stage area. As she walks she sprays, and reads in a serious tone. She sprays the perfume on objects and into the air above the
audience's heads. She goes over to where Claire the artist is sitting
and sprays over her head too.

                    RACHEL

    The smell of fresh grass cuttings releases tension.
    SerenaScent is the result of a seven-year project by Dr. Nick
    Lavidis and Professor Rosemarie Einstein at the University of
    Queensland in Australia.

Dr. Lavidis explains: 'This perfume recreates chemicals that directly impact on the amygdala and the hippocampus parts of the brain. These two areas are responsible for the flight or fight response and the endocrine system, which controls the releasing of stress hormones such as corticosteroids. The solution appears to regulate these two areas.'

Since September 2011 this is being tested on Death Row prisoners in the Huntsville Unit, Texas, where SerenaScent is dispensed through the ventilation system into prison cells. The results show an increase of reading by inmates and a decrease in masturbation. Also I'm to inform you the dog is a passive indicator dog. This means she is trained to be non-aggressive, not to bark, or have any physical contact with you. She will stand still and stare at a person in the room exuding strong fear pheromones. Please note this may also indicate a person who is extremely empathetic.

Rachel goes to the stage area and puts down the spray bottle and places the script in her bag. She picks up the canisters and lids, the packets of gauze pads, pen and contracts and puts them in the over-sized bag. Rachel moves to the off-stage area and buys a drink. Ten minutes later the dog handler enters with the dog. Rachel follows their movement. The dog makes a find.

DOG HANDLER (TO VOLUNTEER)

We have been employed to track fear pheromones. You have been selected by the dog because you are exuding strong fear pheromones. Please talk to the presenter about this, there may be a job for you.

The dog and handler leave the room. Rachel approaches the volunteer chosen by the dog. This section to be memorised.

RACHEL (INSTRUCTING THE VOLUNTEER)

Are you happy to collect your fear pheromones? I will go 50-50 on any money I make from them.

Rachel talks while removing canister, lid and packet of gauze pads from over-sized handbag.

                              RACHEL

    Maybe go to the toilet cubicle with this canister and use
    these --

Rachel hands over the gauze pads.

                              RACHEL

    -- to wipe underarms, palms of hands, and back of knees.
    Thanks. Find me when you come out. I have a contract for you
    to sign and keep. Also you will receive £20.00 for your par-
    ticipation in today's event.

The volunteer enters the toilet cubicle. Volunteer wipes the body
with gauze pads provided and deposits the samples into the canister.
Volunteer removes the semtex paper hidden inside the rim of his/her
sock and adds to canister. The volunteer removes footwear and the con-
taminated sock, presses sock into the canister, wipes shin and hands
with the antiseptic gel, takes clean sock out of bag and puts on foot
followed by footwear. The volunteer next twists the tamper evident lid
onto canister, drops antiseptic gel into bag and exits the toilet with
canister in hand.

The volunteer finds the presenter and returns the canister. Presenter
and volunteer sign two contracts. Presenter keeps one copy of the contract and gives the other with money attached to the volunteer.

Presenter inserts the canister into the stamped addressed envelope and
places it on the speaker. Presenter mingles with visitors while watching for the dog's next entrance.

The dog enters 15 minutes later to make another find. The process is
repeated (three times in total). If next artist is in agreement, dog
and handler enter during the next presentation/event.

End of presenter's script.

Post event:

• Artist ensures the dog handler, volunteers and presenter are paid the
agreed fees.

• Artist asks the volunteers to hide the airtight containers containing
latex gloves behind the toilet cistern.

• Artist collects the over-sized bag from the presenter and collects boxes from behind toilet cistern.

• Artist stores in over-sized bag: canisters (containing gauze pad pheromone samples, semtex paper, sock); one full script; one purse with money; one set of keys; one deodorant stick; serenascent perfume; one lighter; latex gloves in airtight container and one change of clothes.

• Artist adds a contract to two of the envelopes containing canisters.

• Artist locates a post box and sends these two stamped addressed envelopes to DARPA.

• Artist loses the over-sized bag on a train/bus on her way home. Artist reports the missing bag and its contents to lost property. If found artist requests lost property to produce an inventory of the items in the bag.

Visitor Employment Contract

The following shall constitute a contract of employment made on 14 February 2012, between herein referred to as VISITOR, and RACHEL COCKBURN herein referred to as PRESENTER.

SECTION 1: EMPLOYMENT OF VISITOR
VISITOR hereby engages to collect sweat pheromones at The Showroom Gallery, London NW8 8PQ and VISITOR hereby accepts such employment on the terms set forth in this contract.

SECTION 2: TERMS OF EMPLOYMENT
The term of employment shall be on the day and times here specified: 14 February 2012, 18:30 to 21:00 hours.

SECTION 3: COMPENSATION
In consideration of the VISITOR's services, PRESENTER agrees to pay the VISITOR £20.00, to be paid by Rachel Cockburn at the conclusion of the event at which VISITOR has actually worked. If VISITOR fails to produce any sweat pheromones or is incapacitated from rendering the act through sickness or otherwise, the VISITOR shall not receive any compensation.

SECTION 4: DUTIES OF THE VISITOR
VISITOR shall provide his/her services in a competent manner, and perform at times specified by PRESENTER, abide by all reasonable rules and requirements that PRESENTER shall make, and as long as VISITOR fully performs his/her obligations hereunder, render services exclusively for PRESENTER during the term of this contract.

SECTION 5: PUBLICITY
Clip art and other promotional material will be available to view on Claire Makhlouf Carter's Facebook account within six months of the event taking place. Web site: http://www.facebook.com/clairemakloufcarter

SECTION 6: SALES OF FEAR PHEROMONES
PRESENTER agrees to offer for sale the fear pheromones collected from VISITOR's body if provided by VISITOR. VISITOR agrees to allow PRESENTER to retain 50 per cent (50%) of all net sales of VISITOR's fear pheromones sold to any third parties. PRESENTER will assume the cost of postage to and from DARPA, Defense Advanced Research Projects Agency, Virginia 22203–1714, USA.

SECTION 7: DOCUMENTATION OF EVENTS

Where VISITOR's employment at the event is recorded, in whole or in part, VISITOR releases PRESENTER and her 'employee' to use such recordings for its archives only. If VISITOR's employment is recorded for other purposes, PRESENTER and employee do not agree to obtain an additional release from VISITOR prior to the use of any such documentation.

SECTION 8: TERMINATION

Either party may terminate this contract by giving the other party at least five (5) minutes verbal notice to be witnessed by a third party. This contract shall automatically terminate without further notice at the end of the term of employment as specified in SECTION 2.

SECTION 9: INDEMNIFICATION

PRESENTER does not agree to indemnify VISITOR against all loss or damage that VISITOR may suffer as a result of being engaged by PRESENTER. In witness whereof, the parties have executed this contract, the date and year first above written.

Presenter   Visitor

....
Signature   Signature

....
Print   Print

Volunteer Schedule

Criodhna	Frank	Nancy	
18:00	18:15	18:25	Meet outside the gallery. Surreptitiously drop in bag: airtight container containing Semtex paper, latex gloves and antiseptic hand gel.
18:10	20:40	20:20	Enter toilet cubicle — put on gloves and insert Semtex paper securely in the rim of your sock. Place gloves in airtight container and place in bag.
20:10	20:50	20:30	Dog enters the room, searches for Semtex — stands and stares at you. Dog handler rewards dog with tennis ball and recites a statement to you. Presenter gives instructions. Agree. Without delay go to the bathroom with white canister and gauze pads. Remove Semtex and sock and place in white canister with the gauze pads (see script for details). Exit bathroom. Follow presenter's instructions. Presenter pays your expenses.

Commissioned for an artist's talk, *Archival Pleasure* with Melissa Gronlund and Paul Buck, The Showroom, 14.6.11, and the exhibition *The Artist Talks*, The Showroom, 18.4.12 to 2.6.12.

The artist talks: script for a performance
Sarah Pierce

An artist sits at the front of a room or lecture hall facing the audience. After being introduced to the audience by another party, she/he reads the following text; after the text is read through once, the artist repeats it, reading it the same way and performing the accompanying gestures. Do not read out the names of the artists associated with each part. The host introduces the artist to the audience in a customary manner.

PART A: DORA GARCÍA

ARTIST

Thanks you and to all. I was thinking not make it too tedious I was going to select from five projects and tell a bit about them and then maybe through Gavin and through Jane we ask questions and through all of you of course. I'm thinking that I could start with two old projects in time.

Put glasses on.

One of course is the one we were talking about ... eh ... where is it? ... I'm sorry ... of course ... now I don't know where it is ... here it is. Eh exactly. So eh, 'All the Stories' weblog. So this is sort of a hobby started in 1999 which was about a collection of stories.

Remove glasses.

So I started to think about ... well it came from a book called, I think, 'How to Write a Good Script' and then I started to see examples of what is called pitch ... when you propose a film to Hollywood the first contact you have with a producer is ... cannot be longer than four lines and then on those four lines they decide if it's worth to keep talking to you or not. So I thought it would be nice to reduce down all the stories to these four lines and try to count them. Knowing a bit in this idea of course that every day, every second new stories are created and so this kind of impossible task is something that is present in many works ... I started counting them. And counting and telling them in Spanish is the same words, countar, to count and to tell, eh ... and then to see how far how far you get ...

PART B: SLAVS AND TATARS

ARTIST

Thank you. Thank you to the Eastside Projects and Book Works team for inviting us both for the show and for this um for this eh artist talk. Um the talk tonight is focusing on, on books and archives and how they work in our practice. It wouldn't be an understatement to say that sort of everything, everything for us starts with books in a sense. Insofar as my books are far away from me right now they're in Moscow in this building here, where, where half of the Slavs and Tatars library is. These are one of Stalin's seven sisters. Um. They're called Stalin's seven sisters because there're seven of them in Moscow that sort of, that uh, that uh, work as landmarks in that city which otherwise doesn't really have any landmarks. Stalin built these in a sense to show the Americans that they're not, they're not the only ones who had skyscrapers in the fifties. And so they are this interesting mash up of neoclassical, Stalinist and kind of, and uh, and Gothic very much inspired by sort of what you see on Central Park West, and Dakota building. Um also for me they remind me kind of of 'big middle finger' which is what Stalin was trying to say to America --

Raise arm and wave middle finger back and forth in front of audience.

Kind of with a big spire in the middle? Um and uh, and when you walk into these buildings you feel like you're kind of Batman or Elliot Ness, I mean, they're uh, they're quite majestic and show the kind of inferiority -- slash -- superiority complex that Russians and big countries often have I think. Um, these are just some images of the library, in Moscow, um and I'm very happy that Andre has joined us tonight who helped us catalogue this library over the last couple of months in Moscow ...

PART C: JONATHAN MONK

ARTIST

Good afternoon. Um, quite strange that ... anyway. Em ... I
decided when asked to do a talk about books that I wouldn't
actually bring any books with me. Em ... these aren't mine.
But I, I eh, thought it was kind of more interesting to talk
about this idea of eh, bookmaking and maybe book collecting or
books in general, um so I took some photographs, when I knew
they had this, this machine ...

Wave arm horizontally over the desk.

... Em. It's slightly delayed, eh that I could take some photographs, of my studio and eh, kind of library, a bit grand
to say it's a library because it's a complete mess, um. And
instead of showing a kind of classic talk about eh, I don't
know, books and bookmaking, I thought it was maybe more interesting to show the books that have perhaps influenced what I
do, rather then the end product. Um, so I took a lot of photographs, which I'll now show you. This is eh, I live in Berlin
actually, but I was, I'm from Lester. Which is not far from
here. Well, it's quite far. Em, so this is where I kind of
work. In this room here. Um, I made a little sculpture there
of the word 'book', actually. And this is eh, I guess there
are things in the studio, and in the house that somehow influence what I do. And eh, that's really, kind of, my idea of
doing the talk ...

Repeat all parts, A to C.

...with two old projects in time. PUT GLASSES ON. One of course is the one we were talking... Thanks you and to all. I was thinking not to make it too tedious I was going to select from five projects and tell a bit about them and then maybe through Gavin and through Jane we ask questions and through all of you of course. I'm thinking but... So this is sort of a hobby started in 1999 which was about... which I could start... So I started to think about... So I started to Hollywood the first contact you have with a producer is... cannot be longer than... collection of stories. REMOVE GLASSES. So I started to think about... well it came from a book called, I think, how to write a good script and then I started to see examples of what is called Pitch... when you propose a film to you or not. So I thought it would be nice to... where is it?... I'm sorry... of course... now I don't know where it is... here it is. Eh exactly. ...of course... four lines and then on those four lines they decide if it's worth to keep talking to you or not... them. Knowing a bit in this idea of course that every day, every second new stories are created and so... to reduce down all the stories to this four lines and try to count them... this kind of impossible task is something that is... present in many works... I started counting them. And counting and telling them in Spanish is the same words, contar, to count and to tell, eh... and then to see how far you go...

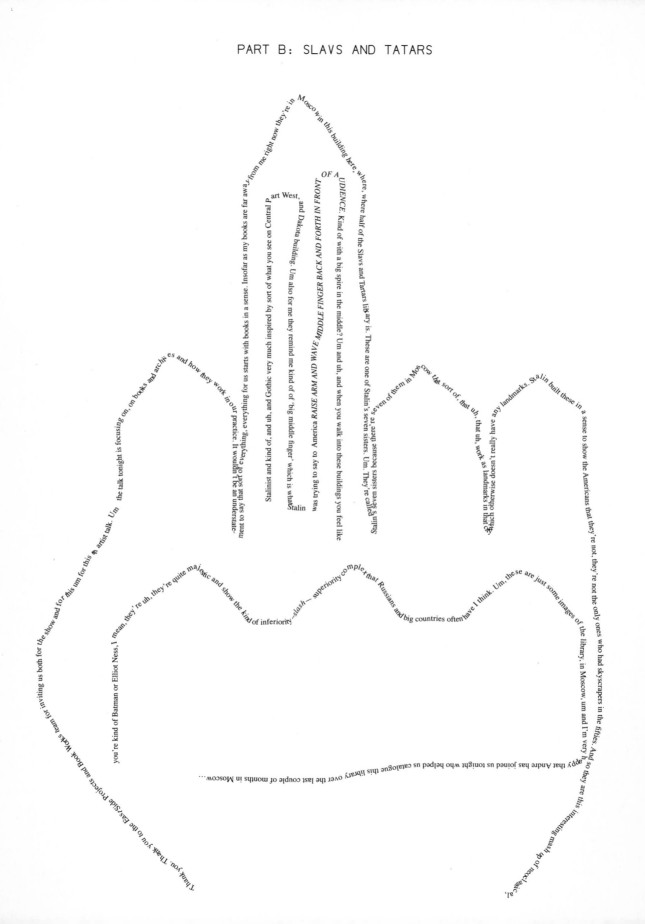

Thank you. Thank you to the EastSide Projects and Book Works team for inviting us both for the show and for this um for this an artist talk. Um the talk tonight is focusing on, on books and archives and how they work in our practice. It wouldn't be an understatement to say that sort of everything, everything for us starts with books in a sense. Insofar as my books are far away from me right now they're in Moscow in this building here, where, where half of the Slavs and Tatars library is.

Stalinist and kind of, and uh, and Gothic very much inspired by sort of what you see on Central Park West, and Dakota building. Um also for me they remind me kind of of 'big middle finger' which is what Stalin was trying to say to America *RAISE ARM AND WAVE MIDDLE FINGER BACK AND FORTH IN FRONT OF AUDIENCE.* Kind of with a big spire in the middle? Um and uh, and when you walk into these buildings you feel like

These are one of Stalin's seven sisters. Um. They're called Stalin's seven sisters because there are, there are seven of them in Moscow. the sort of, that uh, that uh, work as landmarks in that — which otherwise doesn't really have any landmarks. Stalin built these in a sense to show the Americans that they're not, they're not the only ones who had skyscrapers in the fifties. And so they are this interesting mash up of neoclassical,

you're kind of Batman or Elliot Ness, I mean, they're uh, they're quite majestic and show the kind of inferiority —slash— superiority complex that Russians and big countries often have I think. Um, these are just some images of the library, in Moscow, um and I'm very happy that Andre has joined us tonight who helped us catalogue this library over the last couple of months in Moscow....

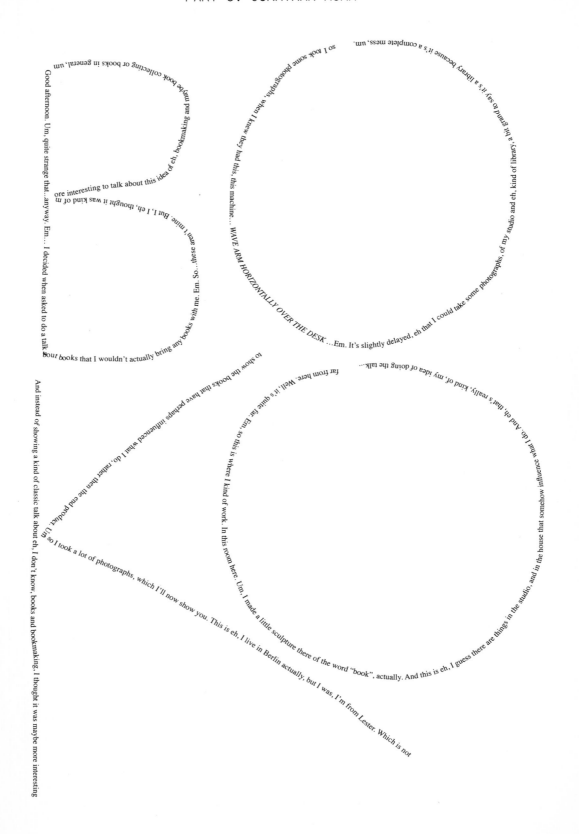

Good afternoon. Um, quite strange that...anyway. Em.... I decided when asked to do a talk about books that I wouldn't actually bring any books with me. Em. So...these aren't 'mine'. But I, I eh, thought it was kind of more interesting to talk about this idea of eh, bookmaking and maybe book collecting or books in general, um

so I took some photographs, when I have w, they had this, this machine.... WAVE ARM HORIZONTALLY OVER THE DESK...Em. It's slightly delayed, eh that I could take some photographs, of my studio and eh, kind of library, a bit grand to say it's a library because it's a complete mess, um...

far from here. Well, it's quite far. Em, so this is where I kind of work. In this room here. Um, I made a little sculpture there of the word "book", actually. And this is eh, I guess there are things in the studio, and in the house that somehow influence when what I do. And eh, that's really, kind of, my idea of doing the talk....

to show the books that have perhaps influenced what I do, rather then the end product. Um so I took a lot of photographs, which I'll now show you. This is eh, I live in Berlin actually, but I was, I'm from Lester. Which is not

And instead of showing a kind of classic talk about eh, I don't know, books and bookmaking, I thought it was maybe more interesting

Text of presentation reprinted after event, *Confrontational Perspectives*, night of confrontations, performances and readings from a feminist perspective, with Claire Makhlouf Carter, Marina Vishmidt and Chicks on Speed, commissioned for *Again, A Time Machine*, The Showroom, 14.2.12.

Risky analogies: the order of disruption in feminist art and feminist politics

Marina Vishmidt

In the short text that has been circulated announcing the topics of my talk tonight, the term 'negative critique' is used. Why 'negative'? Isn't there a dimension of negativity in all critique, in fact, in all questioning, which may or may not take the structured form of critique? The reason 'negative' is there as a modifier of critique is to introduce the possibility of a heuristic distinction, that between positive critique, which has the purpose of basically salvaging and rehabilitating its object into a more desirable state, and negative critique, which aims at the dissolution of its object, but also at the dissolution of the conditions which make it possible, hence aiming at its impossibility as well as at a cessation of its existence under current conditions.

The second implication of this distinction is that the positive critique would ideally wish to secure its own conditions of existence, namely, to bring about a state of the situation in which its proposals are no longer critical of the establishment but *are* the establishment, where they can emerge in their true world-making capacity, or at least have their advisory capacity legitimated by power in some way, have their power recognised. The negative critique includes itself in the conditions it would wish to see abolished, guided by the idea that so long as the current situation (patriarchy, capitalism, exploitation) perseveres, we cannot even concretely imagine what kind of life and society would be made possible by their abolition. Yet to paint these two discursive formations as antithetical or principally opposed — constructive vs. destructive, reform vs. revolution — is not that revealing. Not only because actual practices of critique, while being oriented more or less in one of these directions, each include a moment, or moments of the other, but this 'dialectic' is evinced in the very constitution of struggle: no purely negative, or purely utopian, perspective has ever been sufficient to trigger large transformative social movements or historical revolution — while struggling to improve a position in the current society, it may become clear that neither the position nor the society is tenable, i.e. likely to produce this outcome. It is also the case that positive critique — the form of the demand addressed to an authority endowed with power, located somewhere in the fabric of governance — can in the course of a movement turn more towards the negative, as the material practices of revolt, and the response of the state, bring with them their own logic of escalation and generalisation. This is something that is very clear from observing, for example, the revolutions in Tunisia or Egypt, as well as the trajectory of Occupy Oakland, and the Occupy phenomenon more synthetically. But this is of course not a debate, tactical or theoretical, which is happening in the field of 'pure politics', as many, including many within the Occupy movement, would like to depict it: deteriorating material conditions are just as, if not more, efficient in tipping positive critique into negative, as the example of Greece shows, not to say the role of foreclosure, unemployment and intolerable levels of debt in driving people to assent to and participate in Occupy in the US.

However, what I would like to focus on here is more how we can translate the terms of negative and positive critique into terms we can use to analyse what I'll call structural invariants in feminist history and the art practices that associated, or continue to associate themselves, with feminist politics of one sort or another. When I say structural invariants, I mean primarily those of identification and dis-identification with the category of 'woman' as a political, philosophical or existential category. Here, I am interested primarily in how the category of gender can act in similar, and also very disjunctive ways, to the category of class, how gendered labour and labour as such start to emerge as categories of social being to be abolished, insofar as both are enforcement mechanisms of social subordination and economic exploitation. Further, how the category of woman naturalises certain kinds of labour and its relation, or non-relation, to wages which acts as a sort of social contract between autonomous persons and the labour that they sell. Historically this is a contract which women, as women, have not had access to, or access to only on unfavourable terms compared to the normalised subject (male, white, skilled) of waged labour.

The poet and philosopher Denise Riley, in her book, *'Am I That Name'? Feminism and the Category of 'Women' in History*, explores how the feminist movement has always had to deal with the central contradiction that it had to affirm the category of women as a distinct social group with specific disadvantages and qualities in order to overturn this category in the current organisation of society. This of course had different consequences for the various political affiliations and schools of thought that developed within second-wave feminism and which resonate into the present, like radical feminism, separatism, liberal or equality feminism, materialist feminism, socialist feminism, etc. This operates in a similar way to class, how in the historical materialist framework, the working class, as the class embodying the contradictions of capitalist society, must abolish itself in order to effect a revolutionary overcoming of class society. How not to identify with the structural role allotted to you by power while leveraging that role to question and upset the whole premise of the system, that is the structure of 'radical identification'? There is always a dialectic of affirmation and negation, and insofar as this dialectic is thwarted, or the movement decomposes, we have the stagnation and crystallisation of categories of struggle into sociological or cultural categories, for example the cultural concept of class belonging, which are essentially categories of administration. These are questions that could be posed philosophically with terms such as identity, negativity, universality, and outline the central problematic of what later came to be called identity politics, and the claims that these lost a radical horizon in petitioning for accommodation within the existing state of things. This could also be linked to the tenet that runs through much current French political philosophy, for example: both Jacques Rancière and Alain Badiou, have theorised that the only possible change has to come from dis-identification with the situation, which also means dis-identification with political identities or collectivities that reproduce the 'logic of the situation', that is, staking a political identity on oppression and liberation for and as the oppressed. How does this interact with social movements where identity was affirmed as ground for re-invention (feminist separatism, Black nationalism, etc.), sometimes as a transitional stage of articulation with larger/long-term movements for social change based on overcoming capitalism/patriarchy/racism? For Rancière, the epitome of this 'dis-identification' or dis-placement, which ties into the earlier point about breaking with the reproduction of affective and social positions that the hegemonic order has decreed, is the instance of the nineteenth-century French workers who, rather than being content with their roles as labourers, wanted to partake in the culture that the bourgeois right had decreed as universal, in this way challenging the distribution of humanity and the premises of universality itself in that society. They negated labour by staying up all night to write poetry. But this notion of 'dis-identification' should also be weighed in all its contradictoriness and contingency, since it can engender a very different kind of movement, a movement to lay claim to the existing structure without changing it, or, put another way, the application of universality without regard for structural inequity, the 're-distribution' of the existing sensible. We can refer to Marx where he discusses the outlawing of trade unions after the French Revolution under 'conspiracy' laws that prohibited the associations of people in 'similar ranks or occupations', since they impeded the 'liberty, equality and fraternity' of the new Republic, establishing for Marx why it was a bourgeois revolution — much as Rancière bans political economy from his own political philosophy, perhaps.

Here we would also need to consider the decomposing influence of feminism itself within class-based social movements, the role which it — and other struggles predicated on identity-based exploitation, such as civil rights, Native American and Black Power movements and Queer Liberation — played in siting politics in the quotidian and affective registers of social and interpersonal life; what has been called 'revolution within the revolution' and the writing on the 'human strike'. Finally here I'd like to briefly mention the redefinition of housework, care work, etc. as productive labour in the 1970s by the autonomist feminists such as Mariarosa Dalla Costa, Selma James, Silvia Federici, Leopoldina Fortunati, etc., which is the perspective that underlay the Wages for Housework demand.

These feminist activists and theorists were responsible for pointing out the necessity of unpaid labour to the system of production dependent on waged labour. This argument can be seen as addressing surplus value production (the dependence of profit on unpaid labour) from the viewpoint of divisions within the working class, that is, from a revolutionary perspective that aims to fashion unity between fractions of the class exploited in very different ways. The wage divides workers from one another and produces a form of discipline and identification between the interests of labour and capital (though it should be noted that the wage preserves a dialectical mismatch between those interests, while the prevalence of debt today coercively closes the gap where that mismatch can become a site of struggle). The solution of collectivising housework and care work would here also be insufficient, as long as the gendered division of waged and unwaged labour, and its place in the larger capital-labour relation, remained unchanged. The strategic importance of re-defining 'women's work' as productive work in terms of capital, was also important, since male 'productive workers' were the most radical and mobilised part of the Italian worker's movement. This was a way to both unite the feminist movement with them — to bring together the feminist and the workers' movement on the ground of exploitation — and to expand the workers' movement into social reproduction, as also seen from the phenomena of self-reduction, proletarian shopping, mass squatting, and so forth. It also enacted the discourse of 'refusal of work', while pointing out that a housewives' strike had a very different meaning from a strike in the factory: a house-work strike would inevitably be more radical, since the withdrawal of labour at the factory relied in great measure on continued labour in the home.

> … by recognising that what we call 'reproductive labour' is a terrain of accumula-tion and therefore a terrain of exploitation, we were able to also see reproduction as a terrain of struggle, and, very important, conceive of an anti-capitalist struggle against reproductive labour that would not destroy ourselves or our communities … This has allowed a re-thinking of every aspect of everyday life — child-raising, relationships between men and women, homosexual relationships, sexuality in general — in relation to capitalist exploitation and accumulation.
> Silvia Federici.

Ultimately, 'excessive demands' and Wages for Housework, although positioned in its historical context and political moment, confront us as inadequate then, and more so now, when it is the disjuncture between labour and the means of reproduction, from the side of capital as well as labour, which needs to be pushed, not resolved, in a way inevitably favour-able to capital and state. The subjective dis-identification with labour and gender cannot take on a positive valence of 'excess' (if we claim the promise of the system that is not intended for us, we will expose the lie of the system), which can only be normalising under the current conditions of normalised disaster, but can help disclose the imperative of negation as a practi-cal politics. It is not simply that the particular strategy of 'excess (wage-) demands' worked in some fashion as a radical politics in the welfare-state Fordist era and is no longer capable of doing so; it is that capital is confronting us with these demands now, the demands that pre-suppose 'conditions where it can no longer be raised'.

It could be ventured that the problem here can also be seen in that the use-value of housework is never questioned in the Wages for Housework demand, (or any demand equat-ing labour and payment, the registration of activity as labour so that it can be recognised in payment): meaning it can become a capitalist commodity with a use-value and an exchange-value like any other, whereas if use-value itself were put under the critical knife, housework as a natural given lying outside the capital-labour relation, essential for reproducing that relation but not commodifiable in its terms, would start to seem as weird a thing to perform for a wage as factory work, or marketing. This is part of why I'm interested in analysing housework in conjunction with post-object art practices, going back, for instance, to the Maintenance Art Manifesto and performances of American artist Mierle Laderman Ukeles, which took place roughly at the same time as Workerist or Autonomist feminism — this was actually housework performed as art inside the museum, and was both implicated in and anticipated a milieu of work and services being reinscribed not just as possible material for, but as the very substance of what was then ludicrously but suggestively called dematerialised art, much as they talk about immaterial labour now.

Crossing over with Wages for Housework in this discussion, I'll also briefly mention W.A.G.E., which campaigns for the financial compensation (in institutional budgets, mainly) for artistic practices that don't produce results and that are easy to reify institutionally or economically: they want 'capitalist value' in return for the 'critical value' they provide, thus hoping to break the magic link between artists and speculators subjectively and structurally. The reply to this could of course be the same as the point being made throughout this paper: that is how to demand improved conditions of reproduction under conditions which themselves need to be eradicated. As Paolo Virno says with reference to the above, 'Nowadays artistic labour is turning into wage labour while the problem is, of course, how to liberate human activity in general from the form of wage labour'. Thus it is worth, as I attempt to do in my more art-oriented research, to separate these levels out a bit and try to claim not the similarity of art to life as radical, but the *mimetic* relation — with 'mimetic' referring to a notion of mimesis that can be derived, in different ways, from the work of Theodor Adorno, Walter Benjamin, and Roger Callois. Further, I would say that it doesn't make a lot of sense to look at the relation between art and politics without first seeing how art and labour diverge and converge in capital.

I would like to conclude by considering two further art practices, one historical and one contemporary, that perform negative critique of labour and gender by infiltrating the social spaces where the normative identities associated with these categories are reproduced and disrupt the affective and semiotic economies of those spaces. Just like the staging of women's work as a political category tends to undermine the logic of both the gender and the labour aspect of that term, women's artwork can be undertaken as a critique of both the artistic subject, artistic work, and the system of values they circulate in. This, then, would constitute the parallel to 'revolution within the revolution' in politics, and is something Griselda Pollock has written about extensively:

> All these moves radically challenged what art was thought to be, breaking the
> modernist myth that art was a separate realm, apart from society and immune
> to politics and power … I think we owe it to the women of the 1970s and early
> 1980s to come to appreciate and understand what they have done to the very
> possibilities of art as part of women's political struggle.

This talk was interrupted by the author after 20 minutes, and the film,
'From the Reports of Security Guards and Patrol Services No. I', 1984,
by Helke Sander was screened.

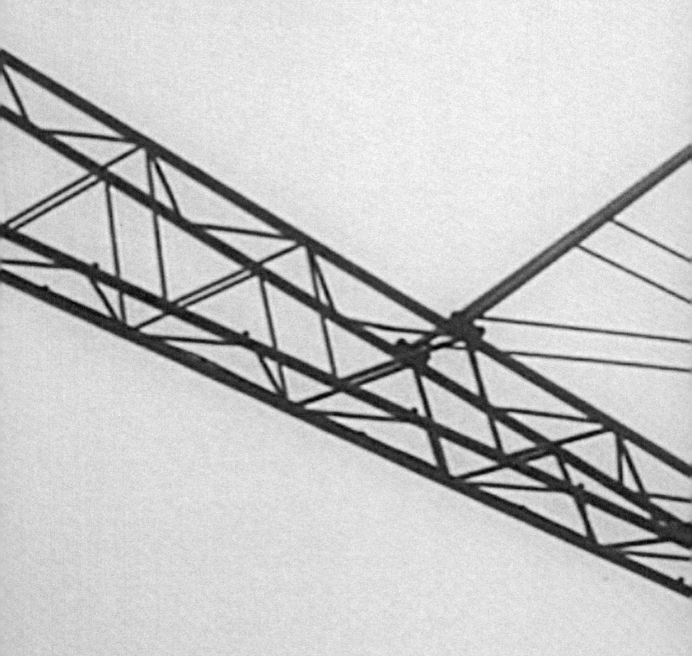

The early approaches to combining a politics of women's work and artwork are often discussed in terms of craft, and bringing de-valued, vernacular expressions of women's reproductive or decorative labour into the 'fine art' milieu. This is by and large historicised as coming into conflict with postmodernist feminist art, which was more concerned with social, sexual and 'psychic difference' than a purported 'essence' of female identity in Western capitalist societies. But we need to be clear that this is something of an over-schematised and reductive account. As Arlene Raven writes in the catalogue to the 1995 exhibition *Division of Labor: 'Women's Work' in Contemporary Art*:

> What I call the 'dichotomy of the decades' — the essentialist / deconstruction-ist debate — in feminist theory and practice has been hyperbolised as well as misinterpreted. Early feminist efforts were neither 'essential' nor simplistic ... but environmentally and conceptually complex. Completely new forms and new relationships between forms were invented, fusing the implications of the female body with man-made structures about femininity, and educating, then driving the viewer to action rather than mere contemplation.

There is also the modality of media and ideology critique of the performance of gender as a commodity and an eroticised edifice of discipline, which artists as various as Hannah Wilkes and Sanja Ivekovic engaged in. Then there were the complicated and rigorous later positions, such as Rosemarie Trockel's, that took a formalist approach to the tropes of the aesthetics of ideology as manifested in state and gender doctrine, for example in her late '80s works of blankets embroidered with the hammer and sickle. So here again is the question of identification and dis-identification, a dramatising of the division of labour by gender and also between labour (or 'craft') and art, and how value is differentially operated across them.

In Raven's quote, there is of course another essentialised dichotomy deployed between action and mere contemplation that itself indicates a direction for art practice that uses its capacity as an un- or under-determined form of social practice to alienate the protocols of social spaces, including art spaces, from both acceptable modes of functioning as a viewer, active and passive, to interfere in the 'benignity' of the social space of sanctioned experimentation, which current practitioners such as Mattin, Emma Hedditch, or Claire Makhlouf Carter, here today, try to implement. I am also thinking of Adrian Piper, in her '70s performance works where she violated the social protocols of alienated public space with the physical expression of a more extreme alienation (towel stuffed in mouth on public transport, walking the street with clothes covered in diverse spatters), which was interesting both in breaking the social contract of how a woman, and especially a black woman, was supposed to conduct herself in public (docility of the governed subject) and in anticipating / embodying the social dislocation of the neoliberal shift to come, when encounters with mentally and socially dislocated people (the homeless in Manhattan, for example) would become such a common-place feature of urban space that her interventions would probably have gone unnoticed. The refusal of the female identity of necessity harbours a moment of articulation of that identity. Identification can be resisted as a strategy of control; conversely, refusal of all identification can also mean quietism and internal exile. It is rather the space where identification is performed, authorised or broken which may be more relevant.

Marianne Wex's photographic archive and book *Let's Take Back Our Space* (1972–77) comes at the highpoint of the second-wave feminist movement, and speaks out of a feminist culture. As a piece of activist research, it is emphatic: she is compiling an exhaustive catalogue of gesture to illustrate what the impact of patriarchy is on the body. The subtitle cites 'female' and 'male' body language, with the single quotes already summing up the project's hypothesis: gender is not given but constructed by historically specific social relations. Physical behaviour is unconscious, and, as Jacques Lacan remarked of the unconscious, it is 'structured like a language'. Like Mary Kelly's *Post-Partum Document* (1973–79), another piece of austere taxonomic art that came out of the feminist movement roughly around the same time, the invocation of language as mediating purportedly natural identities like 'woman' or 'mother' is utterly crucial, and the concept of language is an expansive one: for Wex, it includes how bodies are held in space, for Kelly it includes every way her status as a mother registers socially, from negotiations with nursery schools to keeping a diary of her child's development to the material debris of the mother-child relation.

Am also thinking of Pilvi Takala. Her 2008 video *The Trainee* depicts the Finnish artist embarking upon a placement as a trainee with a marketing company. Initially undertaking the standard array of tasks allotted her in this role, her behaviour starts to subtly shift over time, to the perplexity of her colleagues. After several months, she no longer undertakes any tasks. But instead of enacting a Bartleby-like stance of existential refusal in the workplace, Takala is actually attempting to live up to the tenets of unfettered creativity featured in the rhetoric accompanying her professional development, the tenets of spontaneous and ungovernable value creation that each company must learn how to foster in its employees if it wants to stay ahead of the game. She spends her days sitting at her desk staring into space. Inquiries are met with the singular response, 'I am thinking'.

Here it could be ventured that the artist is dramatising or parodying the capitalisation of attention as labour which has been written about extensively in theories of post-Fordism, along with the 'virtuosity' explored by Virno, all of which bring art as the suspension of labour and labour as the suspension of creativity, closer together to the point of indistinction, flowing into a common mode of 'process over product'. In *The Trainee*, art acts as a magnifying lens for the suspension of labour as integral to the actuality of contemporary work: the disposition, the readiness to work, is already the chief affective and subjective requirement of today's abstract labour. Thinking might already be labour, might already be attention subsumed to the regime of valorisation, but it might also be just thinking, or nothing — clearly Takala's on-the-job performance did not serve to advance her marketing career (this might have also pertained to her lowly status as trainee — perhaps had she attained to an executive post, her claim to be 'thinking' as work might have been given more credence). While it is not uncommon for motifs appropriated from or emulating the world of labour to infiltrate art over the past several decades, if not earlier, with the Productivists and Constructivists, Takala's piece is perhaps one of a small number that try to represent the changes to the experience and expectations of work in recent times — which can be summed up as its unrepresentability, its loss of definition. Of course, there are other ways for art to register these changes that are not representational but also, or instead, structural — these are the more 'invisible', relational or performative practices I have discussed elsewhere.

This publication was produced in response to, and as an extension of, the touring exhibition in six parts, *Again, A Time Machine*, 2011–12. We would like to thank all the artists, writers, curators, designers, gallery staff, audiences, and indeed everyone who participated in this project, for their contributions.

Particular thanks are due to our partners and co-curators whom we worked with in each venue: Gavin Wade (Eastside Projects); Alexis Zavialoff (Motto, Berlin); Emily Pethick (The Showroom); Marie-Anne McQuay (Spike Island); Matthew Higgs (White Columns) and Paul Pieroni (Space, London); James Langdon for his excellent design work on promotional materials, and publications and printed matter for Slavs and Tatars, Dora García, and Jonathan Monk.

We would like to thank the following for their generous support in funding this project: Arts Council England, Grants for the Arts; The Henry Moore Foundation; Iran Heritage Foundation; Polish Cultural Institute; Sharjah Foundation — Sharjah Biennial 10, 2011; FLAMIN; Institut Français du Royaume-Uni; Culture Ireland; and Mark Pawson for loaning archive material for the Stewart Home archive.

Final thanks are due to all those at Book Works (still there and recently left) who have worked so hard on this project, especially Karen Di Franco, James Brook and Paul Sammut.

Again, A Time Machine programme

Part 1: Eastside Projects, Birmingham
26 February to 16 April 2011
New work by Dora García, Jonathan Monk, and Slavs and Tatars

The Happy Hypocrite, Say What You See
31 March 2011
Co-hosted by An Endless Supply and Maria Fusco, particpipants include a.a.s., Phil Baber, Harry Blackett, Helen Brown, Ben Dawson, Gene-George Earle & Ross Gillard, Karin Kilhberg & Reuben Henry, Kelly Large, Hanne Lippard, Apexa Patel, Nathaniel Pitt, Adam Smythe, Stinky Wizzleteat, and Marie Toseland

Part 2: Motto, Berlin
6 May to 2 June 2011
Book Works archival exhibition, with collaged poster works by James Brook and James Langdon

Motto/Chert Peformance event
13 May 2011
Co-hosted by Sternberg Press and Archive Books, with Gavin Everall and James Brook from Book Works, Simon Fujiwara, Maria Fusco, Stewart Home, Ingo Niermann, Katrina Palmer, Markus Wiesbeck and Niklaus Maak

Part 3: The Showroom, London
Performative talks

Archival Pleasure, 14 June 2011
Paul Buck, Melissa Gronlund and Sarah Pierce

Future Orientation, 5 July 2011
Pil and Galia Kollectiv, Plastique Fantastique and Alexis Zavialoff

Part 4: Spike Island
16 September to 9 October 2011
New work by Laure Prouvost, Dora García, Jonathan Monk, Slavs and Tatars and Book Works Archive; with additional talks by Laure Prouvost and Rory Macbeth, and Book Works, Ian Hunt, and Francesco Pedraglio

Book Works Archive
Make The Living Look Dead
A fictional archive of material from a selection of Book Works' artists:
An Endless Supply, Steve Beard and Victoria Halford, Pavel Büchler, Martin John Callanan, Brian Catling, Adam Chodzko, Jeremy Deller, Mark Dion, Giles Eldridge, Ruth Ewan, Luca Frei, Dora García, Beatrice Gibson and Will Holder, Liam Gillick, Susan Hiller, Karl Holmqvist, Stewart Home, Hanne Lippard, Jonathan Monk, Bridget Penney, Sarah Pierce, Elizabeth Price, Laure Prouvost, Clunie Reid, John Russell, Slavs and Tatars, NaoKo TakaHashi, Nick Thurston, Lynne Tillman, Mark Titchner, Alison Turnbull, Eva Weinmayr, and Neal White

Backward / Forward
Moving image works and sound archive compiled by Karen Di Franco and James Brook

The Happy Hypocrite: Miniature Essay
8 October 2011
Co-hosted by Maria Fusco and Spike Associates, participants include:
David Berridge Julia Carver Homeland, LOW PROFILE, Sam Hasler, Sophie Hope, Bridget Penney, Steven Paige, Francesco Pedraglio, The Piracy Project, Barry Sykes, Clare Thornton and Marie Toseland

Spike Island Artists' Book and Zine Fair
8 October 2011
In association and organised by Spike Island and Spike Associates, participants include:
2HB, Åbäke, AND, Article Press, Banner Repeater, Bedford Press, Book Works, Bridget Crone: Plenty Projects, Gagarin, G39 + WARP, Sophie Hope, Toby Huddlestone, InterCityMainLine, Invisible Books, LemonMelon, Marbled Reams, Motto Berlin, Mute, No Fixed Abode, Novel, Occasional Papers, Steven Paige: Bibliophile, Francesco Pedraglio, Pil and Galia Kollectiv, Magnus Quaife, Torpedo Press, Urbanomic, and Zero Books

Part 5: White Columns, New York
22 October to 19 November 2011
Stewart Home archive, and performance by Stewart Home and Kenneth Goldsmith

Part 6: SPACE, London
6 April to 20 May 2012
Stewart Home archive, and a *Night of Psychedelic Noir* with Stewart Home, Katrina Palmer and Bridget Penney, and screenings of *Master of the Flying Guillotine* and *Scorpion Thunderbolt*

Final part: The Showroom, London
18 April to 2 June 2012
New work by Sarah Pierce, with reappearances by Jonathan Monk, Dora García and the Book Works archive including *Make the Living Look Dead* and *Backward / Forward*

The Artist Talks: Lectures, After Rilke
8 May 2012
Sarah Pierce, Dave Beech, Melissa Gronlund and Grant Watson

Final event: *The Artist Talks: Performance*
2 June 2012
Sarah Pierce with six London based art students

The Happy Hypocrite — Interview
Co-hosted by Maria Fusco and Book Works, participants include: Sam Hasler, Anthony Iles, Hanne Lippard, Jo Melvin, Apexa Patel, Nathaniel Pitt and Jess Thom, Stephen Sutcliffe, and Barry Sykes

Again, A Time Machine ephemera

Designed by James Langdon, Twin typeface by
Mark El-khatib; archive material and ephemera by
Art in Ruins, Paul Buck with Javier Marchán, Alex
Cecchetti, Claire Makhlouf Carter, Chicks on Speed,
Jimmie Durham, Ruth Ewan, Dora García, Mark
Geffriaud, Douglas Gordon, Guerrilla Girls, Victoria
Halford and Steve Beard, Susan Hiller, Stewart
Home, Inventory, Sean Lynch, Jonathan Monk, Chris
Newman, Katrina Palmer, Francesco Pedraglio,
Bridget Penney, Sarah Pierce, Pil and Galia Kollectiv,
Plastique Fantastique, Kit Poulson, Laure Prouvost,
John Russell, Slavs and Tatars, workfortheeyetodo.

Again, A Time Machine printed matter
and publications

Slavs and Tatars, *79.89.09.*, newspaper, designed by
James Langdon, co-published by Book Works and
Eastside Projects, London and Birmingham, 2011

Dora García, *All the Stories*, designed by James
Langdon with Robin Kirkham, co-published by
Book Works and Eastside Projects, London and
Birmingham, 2011

Jonathan Monk, *A Poster Project*, ten posters from
Birmingham, Berlin, Bristol, New York and London,
photography by Stuart Whipps, designed by James
Langdon, published by Book Works, London,
2011–12. Special edition of 45 poster sets, with signed
and numbered photo-collage portrait of Martin
Kippenburger collaged portrait, 2012

Again, A Time Machine publication

Thank you to all the writers and artists who participated in *Again, A Time Machine: from distribution to archive* for contributing to the book; all those who generously contributed to the Why distribute? Why archive? section, or allowed their scripts to be reprinted or revised; and to John Russell and McKenzie Wark for new contributions. For contributing or reading the Book Works conversation, thanks to James Brook, Paul Sammut, Karen Di Franco, James Langdon and Louise O'Hare; Mark El-khatib for customising his Twin typeface for this publication, Gerrie van Noord for proofreading, and James Langdon for his inspirational design.

Front cover image: art work from Pavel Büchler, *Notable Days*, Book Works, London, 1990.

All images courtesy of commissioned artists and authors unless stated otherwise below.

Page 3: Time Machine VOX, from open submission advertisement, 2010; Page 9: Book Works promotional leaflet, 1984; Page 11: Book Works Studio, Borough Market, 1984; Page 12: book launch invitation, Silvia Ziranek, *Very Food*, Book Works, London, 1987; Page 13: letter in support of Book Works, workfortheeyetodo, 1993; Page 14: *Scroll* performance, Brian Catling, The British Library, 1994; Page 15: *From the Ruins*, private view invitation, Art in Ruins and Circle Press, Book Works, 1985; Page 15: *Brown Gives Cash All*, book launch invitation to Chap Books, Andrew Dodds, *Lost in Space*, Siôn Parkinson, *Head in the Railings*, and Eva Weinmayr, *Suitcase Body is Missing Woman*, Book Works, London, 2005; Page 17: book launch invitation, Jeremy Millar, *Confessions*, and David Shrigley, *Err*, Book Works, London, 1995; Page 19: letter from Douglas Gordon to Jane Rolo, 1993; Page 21: new year fax from Imschoot Uitgevers; Page 24: documentation of Guerrilla Girls, as part of *A Women's Perspective*, 1992; Page 26: performance prop; business card with printed text on cardboard, 90 x 51mm, Adrian Piper, *My Calling (Card) #1*, 1986–90, collection of the Adrian Piper Research Archive Foundation Berlin, copyright APRA Foundation Berlin; Page 28: installation, *Make the Living Look Dead*, Spike Island, 2011, photograph by Stuart Whipps; Page 29: contribution to *Make the Living Look Dead*, new archival material, *A Poster Project*, torn, ripped, peeled, An Endless Supply, 2011; Page 31: subscription form, Inventory; Page 32: performance image from *Smash This Puny Existence*, Inventory, 1999; Page 34: *Middlesex Hospital Site from BT Tower*, photograph by Matt Brown, courtesy Flickr/Getty Images; Page 61: contribution to *Make the Living Look Dead*, new archival material, *Red fish, blue fish*, Bridget Penney, 2011; Page 62: live performance, *BALLGAME*, Janice Kerbel, 2011; Pages 70–71: stills from dual-screen rear-projected video installation, *They were. It was that.*, Hannah Rickards, 2009; Pages 74–79: studio images, *some book and tables*, Jonathan Monk, 2012; Page 83: citation, Frantz Fanon, *Wretched of the Earth*, Grove Press, New York, 1963, p.21; Page 114: A Estante bookcase; Page 115: stamp, An Endless Supply, 2012; Page 116: printed matter, The Piracy Project Open Call; Page 119: contribution to *Make the Living Look Dead*, new archival material, *REWRITE*, Karl Holmqvist, 2011; Page 121: Eastside Projects interior drawing by Walter Warton; Page 122–23: *Sell Your Archive* cartoon, Mark Pawson, undated; Page 126: sticker, Publish And Be Damned, 2012; Page 127: reading, Dora García, *All the Stories*, Spike Island, 2011; Page 129: drawing, The Seine Library, 2012; Page 131: installation, Assembly (The Showroom), Agency, 2011; Pages 135–36: front covers, *Update* and *Update #2*, White Columns, 2008 and 2011; Pages 138–55: images, Max Beerbohm, *The Happy Hypocrite*, John Lane, The Bodley Head, London and New York, 1915; Page 162: copies of bills, 1862 and 1866, Centre for Ephemera Study, Department of Typography and Communication Design, University of Reading; Pages 182–85: pages from Lithuanian soldiers' personal scrapbooks, Altyus Afghan War Veterans Museum, Altyus, Lithuania; Pages 206–08: contribution to *Make the Living Look Dead*, new archival material, *The Artist Talks: Dora García, Slavs and Tatars, Jonathan Monk*, Sarah Pierce, 2011; Pages 214–16: film still, *From the Reports of Security Guards & Patrol Services No. 1*, 1984, copyright Helke Sander, and thanks to the Goethe Institute, London.

Again, A Time Machine:
from distribution to archive

Published and distributed by Book Works

ISBN 978-1-906012-40-3

Edited by Gavin Everall and Jane Rolo
Proofread by Gerrie van Noord
Designed by James Langdon
Again Twin typeface by Mark El-khatib
Printed by Die Keure, Bruges

Book Works is funded by Arts Council England,
and this publication is generously supported
by Arts Council England Grants for the Arts and
The Henry Moore Foundation.

  The Henry Moore
Foundation